The Master Keys Series

Unlocking the Mysteries of the Kingdom

SECRETS OF A SERVANT

Glimpses of the Everyday Life of the Apostle Paul

by

Harold McDougal

Secrets of a Servant
Copyright © 2001, 2010 by Harold McDougal
ALL RIGHTS RESERVED

Unless otherwise indicated, all Scripture quotations are from the Authorized King James Version of the Bible.

McDougal Publishing is a ministry of The McDougal Foundation, Inc., a Maryland nonprofit corporation dedicated to spreading the Gospel of the Lord Jesus Christ to as many people as possible in the shortest time possible.

This book was originally published under the title ***Secrets of Success*** © 1990 by Harold McDougal. This is a revised and updated edition.

Published by:

McDougal Publishing
P.O. Box 3595
Hagerstown, MD 21742-3595
www.mcdougalpublishing.com

ISBN 1-58158-045-2

Printed in the United States of America
For Worldwide Distribution

Dedication

To what purpose is this waste?
                                        Matthew 26:8

So said the carnal Pharisees as, in dismay, they watched Mary break the alabaster box containing a pound of very precious and costly ointment called spikenard and, with it, anoint the head and feet of Jesus. What a waste! It could have been sold. It could have been used to improve the living conditions of the poor. It could have been used to support the ministry. Today, nearly two thousand years later, it is still considered a waste to be broken and poured out for Jesus.

I dedicate these pages to those Christians who are not satisfied to be called saints, but who long to be servants, yes, slaves of the Lord Jesus — to be broken, poured out, burned up, wasted, for Him.

Acknowledgments

Every believer would be blessed to have the variety of wonderful family members and friends who serve as advisors and critics that I enjoy. Not only am I deeply indebted to the many godly teachers through whom I have been blessed during many years, but by the living "faithful" who serve as current inspiration and clarification of the truth.

Other Books by Harold McDougal

Principles of Christian Faith

Laying Biblical Foundations

Speaking in Tongues

Who We Are in Christ?

All Things Are Possible

Tokens of His Love

A Note to Bible Lovers

Each one of us has his or her own favorite way of studying the Bible. When I was a new Christian, I was so eager to learn that if a book expressed a truth without giving a Bible reference for it, I was deeply disappointed. I wanted to look everything up, study each point and make it my own. When I began writing myself, I made sure that my writings were well salted with biblical references, and I have never lost that habit. I trust that new Christians as well as mature believers will like the style I have come to love. And for those who want to do additional study, a complete index of scriptural passages can be found at the back of the book.

Contents

Introduction 11

1. A Genuine Conversion 13
2. A Compelling Zeal 21
3. A Recognized Calling 37
4. A Divine Revelation 53
5. A Total Commitment 81
6. A Stubborn Determination 105
7. A Realistic Approach 119
8. A Secret Weapon 135
9. A Life of Faith 141
10. A Man, But What a Man! 151

Index of Bible References Used 165

Introduction

From very early in my Christian experience, I have had a fascination with the life of the apostle Paul. This man became the minister to the Gentiles and established the early Gentile churches. He wrote over half of the New Testament books and through them revealed to us many of the great mysteries of the Kingdom.

In writing to the Romans, Paul stated that through his preaching a mystery had been made known to them which had been kept secret since the world began (see Romans 16:25-26). In writing to the Corinthians, he said, *"Behold, I shew you a mystery"* (1 Corinthians 15:51). When writing to the Ephesians, he asked them to pray for him because he was attempting to *"make known the mystery of the gospel"* (Ephesians 6:18-19).

Of all the early believers, Paul was used in unique ways:

> *God wrought special miracles by the hands of Paul: so that from his body were brought unto the sick handkerchiefs or aprons, and the diseases departed from them, and the evil spirits went out of them.* Acts 19:11-12

Paul, in fact, was used *"more abundantly"* than his fellow apostles:

> *But by the grace of God I am what I am: and his grace which was bestowed upon me was not in vain; but I laboured more abundantly than they all: yet not I, but the grace of God which was with me.* 1 Corinthians 15:10

What an amazing man! We should each emulate his life. For more than fifty years now I have been searching the Scriptures to discover the secrets of Paul's success, and I believe I have discovered some of them. Let me share with you now by way of this book some of the important *Secrets of a Servant* which are revealed to us in the Sacred Scriptures.

Harold McDougal

Chapter 1

A Genuine Conversion

Therefore if any man be in Christ, he is a new creature: old things are passed away; behold, all things are become new.

2 Corinthians 5:17

The metamorphosis of Saul of Tarsus into the apostle Paul is a perfect example of what Christ can do for a man. Not only had he persecuted the Church, but, he wrote:

I imprisoned and beat in every synagogue them that believed on thee. Acts 22:19

> *Beyond measure I persecuted the church of God, and wasted it.*   Galatians 1:13

> *Who was before a blasphemer, and a persecutor, and injurious ...*   1 Timothy 1:13

Paul was an accomplice to murder:

> *Many of the saints did I shut up in prison ... and when they were put to death, I gave my voice against them. And I punished them oft in every synagogue, and compelled them to blaspheme; and being exceedingly mad against them, I persecuted them even unto strange cities.*   Acts 26:10-11

Luke, a companion of Paul in the ministry, said of him:

> *Saul was consenting unto his [Stephen's] death.*
> *And Saul, yet breathing out threatenings and slaughter against the disciples of the Lord, went unto the high priest, and desired of him letters to Damascus to the synagogues, that if he found any of this way, whether they were men or women, he might bring them bound unto Jerusalem.*   Acts 8:1 and 9:1-2

A Genuine Conversion

Paul knew himself better than anyone else did, and he described himself as *"chief"* of sinners (1 Timothy 1:15). But he obtained *"mercy"* (Verse 13) and *"grace"* (Verse 14) because, as he said, *"Christ Jesus came into the world to save sinners"* (Verse 15). God's grace took a man who was *"chief"* of sinners and transformed him into the chief of apostles. Oh, the marvelous miracle of grace that can make a Christian martyr out of a murderer.

In 1964, when I traveled to the Philippines for the first time, I met missionary Olga Robertson and, with her, visited the prisons of that country. There I saw many miracles of God's grace. I saw men who had committed the worst crimes known to society. Many of them were under multiple charges, but through her ministry, a good number had been cleansed by the blood of Jesus and made new.

While I was there, I met an amazing young man and he shared with me his very moving story. Several years before, José Gacusan had killed a policeman in Davao City (a principal city on the island of Mindanao). One of the prison officials, Captain Cariaga, hated Jose. He roughed him up and gave him no food or drink for days. Jose hated the captain in return.

After his trial, Jose was sentenced to life imprisonment and sent to Muntinlupa Prison. He vowed that he would escape and kill Captain Cariaga. It was there in Muntinlupa Prison that he first heard the Gospel message, through the same Olga Robertson. As he heard of the love of Jesus that had nailed his sins to the cross, Jose's hardened heart was touched. He made up his mind to let Jesus make something useful of his torn life. He was marvelously converted and became a real Christian witness around the prison. After a time, he actually became Olga's right-hand man.

About that same time, down in Davao City, the captain happened to go into a Gospel church, heard the message of deliverance, repented of his sins and was saved. It was a notable salvation, for, although he had never been behind bars himself, he had led a wicked life. He later entered the ministry.

Sometime later, the captain contacted Olga to say that he would like to give his testimony in the Muntinlupa Prison for the benefit of the most hardened criminals of the country, and the arrangements were made. When Captain Cariaga entered the prison grounds on the assigned day, a young man approached to help Olga carry some packages of Bibles, song books and instruments. That young man was Jose Gacusan. When the captain and the young man met, they were greatly surprised to see each other. Jose ran and threw his arms around Captain Cariaga. I would love to have

A Genuine Conversion

a picture of that scene. Underneath it I would put a caption — "A Miracle of Love and Grace." It was just such a miracle that transformed Saul of Tarsus, a transformation so complete that not even his name remained the same.

We went back to Muntinlupa several times after Debbie, our first child, was born. We had no reservations about letting Jose hold her. He was no longer a murderer. He was now a real child of God. He had experienced a genuine conversion.

"If any man be in Christ," Paul wrote to the Corinthians years after his own conversion on the road to Damascus, *"he is a new creature: old things are passed away; behold, all things are become new"* (2 Corinthians 5:17). I am troubled by the lack of change in many who claim Jesus Christ as their Lord. Believing in Christ is not a simple mental exercise. It is not just a change of opinion. It is a miracle that produces a total change in us.

I am quite realistic, and I know that many Bible teachings set an ideal for which we are to strive. I haven't found the perfect Christian yet, and I've been looking for a long time now and in many different countries. Although I have met many great men and women, none of them has been perfect.

I'm not expecting perfection, but on the other hand, is it correct to say that we believe in Christ if there has been no change in us, no conversion?

I am positive that it is not. The reason so many of those who call themselves Christians are not effective for the Lord that they have not experienced a genuine conversion. Jesus said:

> *Except ye be converted, and become as little children, ye shall not enter into the kingdom of heaven.* Matthew 18:3

When Peter was preaching soon after the Day of Pentecost, he declared:

> *Repent ye therefore, and be converted, that your sins may be blotted out, when the times of refreshing shall come from the presence of the Lord.* Acts 3:19

I also expect to see the fruits of conversion in those who name the name of Jesus. We cannot be His and remain the same.

Paul instructed Timothy to apply certain requirements for the ministry. Those who ministered should be: *"the husband of one wife," "vigilant," "of good behaviour," "not given to wine," "not a brawler"* and *"[of] a good report of them which are without."* Ministers' wives were expected to be: *"grave, not slanderers, sober, faithful in all things"* (1 Timothy 3:2-12). These

A Genuine Conversion

were all evidences of a genuine conversion experience.

You will never be effective straddling the fence between the flesh and the Spirit, between night and day, between the Church and the world, between sin and righteousness. Get on God's side. Make a clean break with sin. Lay aside compromise, and be a real Christian. Show forth the fruits of a genuine conversion.

This was the first of the secrets Paul taught us through his daily walk with God, and it was an important one. Everything else in our lives hinges on this solid spiritual foundation.

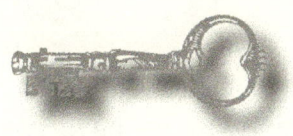

Chapter 2

A Compelling Zeal

And straightway he preached Christ in the synagogues, that he is the Son of God.

Acts 9:20

And he spake boldly in the name of the Lord Jesus, and disputed against the Grecians: but they went about to slay him. Which when the brethren knew, they brought him down to Caesarea, and sent him forth to Tarsus. Then had the churches rest throughout all Judaea and Galilee and Samaria, and were edified; and walking in the fear of the Lord, and in the comfort of the Holy Ghost, were multiplied.

Acts 9:29-31

> *Then departed Barnabas to Tarsus, for to seek Saul: and when he had found him, he brought him unto Antioch. And it came to pass, that a whole year they assembled themselves with the church, and taught much people. And the disciples were called Christians first in Antioch.*
>
> Acts 11:25-26

From Acts 9:31, many have gotten a picture of Paul as an immature believer who was offending so many people with his brashness that he had to be sent home for a time so that everyone could have some peace. It would not be surprising if that had been the case. New believers often have more zeal than tact, and when they finally do learn tact, it is often at the expense of their zeal. Neither seems to have been the case with Paul.

After his conversion, Paul went to Arabia for a time and then returned to Damascus. He caused quite a stir in Damascus, until *"the Jews took counsel to kill him"* (Acts 9:23). They watched the gates day and night so that he could not escape. These men had help from an unexpected quarter. Paul later wrote:

> *In Damascus the governor under Aretas the king kept the city of the Damascenes with a garrison, desirous to apprehend me.*
>
> 2 Corinthians 11:32

A Compelling Zeal

The governor under Aretas, the Arabian king of Petra, was neither a Jew nor a Damascene. Apparently Paul had also stirred up trouble in Arabia, arousing the anger of King Aretas. Aretas sent his governor with a garrison of soldiers, and they set a watch at the gates of Damascus to catch Paul and kill him. So the Jews were watching inside, and the Arabs were watching outside. The Damascene saints took Paul by night, put him in a basket and lowered him from a window between gates on the wall.

Having escaped this very real attempt on his life, Paul went to Jerusalem and attempted to join the other disciples. They had not heard of his conversion, and wondered if this might be a trick. They had heard only of his persecution of the Church.

Barnabas came to Paul's rescue. He was aware of Paul's dramatic conversion, his bold preaching in Damascus and his recent discussions with the Grecians since arriving in Jerusalem. At that very moment these Grecian Jews were already plotting to kill Paul. It seems that Paul was stirring up trouble everywhere he went. When Barnabas introduced these facts to the disciples, they quickly got the picture.

When the disciple named Ananias had gone to Straight Street in Damascus and laid his hands on Paul, Paul's eyes had been opened and he had received the Holy Ghost. Then he was baptized in water, and only then did he eat for the first time in three days and was strengthened. He then spent a few days with the local disciples (see Acts 9:19). Even there in Damascus, Paul immediately began to stir men's hearts:

> *And straightway he preached Christ in the synagogues, that he is the Son of God.*
> Acts 9:20

Paul didn't waste any time, for from the very first day of his conversion to Christ, he had a compelling zeal to declare this Good News. He went right into the Jewish place of worship and began to preach. He had come to that city zealous to persecute the followers of Christ, but he had been changed on his way there. Now he was zealous to promote the way of Christ.

Paul didn't push this responsibility off on the older and more experienced saints of Damascus. He went himself, without fear, and proclaimed to his fellow Jews this message that had transformed his own life.

He was VERY young in the Lord, and he had no seminary training and no knowledge of church government. And certainly he had no license to preach. Yet we read these amazing words:

A Compelling Zeal

> *But all that heard him were amazed, and said; Is not this he that destroyed them which called on this name in Jerusalem, and came hither for that intent, that he might bring them bound unto the chief priests?*
>
> Acts 9:21

The very first time Paul spoke, *"all that heard him were amazed."* They were amazed most of all that the persecutor had turned preacher, the murderer had turned apostle. He who had taken the lives of those who served Christ was now risking his own life for the cause of this man Jesus.

Paul was not satisfied, however, to amaze the people. He wanted to convert the people. He left Damascus and, between verse 22 and verse 23, something wonderful happened to him. He *"increased"* in his spiritual life to the point that he not only amazed the Jews, but *"confounded the Jews which dwelt at Damascus, proving that this is very Christ"* (Acts 9:22).

In verse 23, Paul was back in Damascus and was doing what he was called to do. He had new strength, new wisdom and a new anointing. He spoke with power and authority and was able to prove that Jesus was the Son of God. How was this possible for such a new Christian?

Paul had been in Arabia. How long he was there

and what he was doing there are uncertain. Some have suggested that Paul was in Bible school. In the first chapter of Galatians, however, Paul said that he did not receive the Gospel message from other men. The great change that came to Paul's life leads us to believe that it was during this Arabian visit that he received *"the revelation of Jesus Christ"* (Galatians 1:12). The silence accompanying this period tends to make us believe that Paul was not doing much preaching or many outstanding miracles, but was waiting upon his knees before God, to be taught, strengthened and anointed.

Whatever the case — however long he was there, and whatever he was doing — it established his ministry. He went back to Damascus full of wisdom and power and *"confounded the Jews."* Before this, the Jews had just looked at him in amazement. Now they were spurred to action by his sharp words. They saw that he was a deadly threat to their traditions. Perhaps they saw that he was right and they were wrong. They eventually were so stirred up by what they heard him say that they decided to kill him.

This should not surprise us. The anointed Gospel either draws or repels. It either soothes or incites. It strengthens or it tears down. It heals or it hurts. Paul was thrusting a two-edged sword into the heart of the Jewish people in Damascus, and it cut coming

A Compelling Zeal

and going. And how would they react? Since they would not accept it, they must try to destroy it.

Evidently Paul had not been completely inactive in Arabia. He had done enough to stir up Aretas. And so the Jews and the Arabs, who hated each other, were drawn together through mutual hatred of Christ and Christians, and united to destroy Paul. But God showed Paul a way of escape because his ministry was just beginning.

When Paul arrived in Jerusalem, he did not go into hiding:

> *He spoke boldly in the name of the Lord Jesus.* Acts 9:29

Looking back to chapters six and seven of Acts, we can see a dispute arising between the Hellenistic Jews and Stephen. The Hellenistic Jews were both Europeans and Asiatics who had embraced the culture of the Grecian Empire. Those mentioned in this section were *"the Libertines, and Cyrenians, and Alexandrians and of them of Cilicia and of Asia"* (Acts 6:9).

These Hellenists *"were not able to resist the wisdom and the spirit by which he [Stephen] spake"* (Acts 6:10). They were so angry that *"they suborned [incited to evil] men, which said, We have heard him speak blasphemous words against Moses, and against God"* (Acts

6:11). This stirred up the public in general and the elders and scribes in particular, and they brought Stephen before the council. The Hellenists set up false witnesses against him, but under the anointing of the Holy Ghost, Stephen brought a brilliant defense:

> *When they heard these things, they were cut to the heart and they gnashed on him with their teeth.*　　　　　　　　Acts 7:54

These men were so violent that they were almost like mad animals. They were so bitter against the servant of the Lord that they bit him like mad dogs. But while they were stoning him and biting him, Stephen was looking up to Heaven. He saw Heaven opened, and he saw Jesus standing on the right hand of God. When he said this, it further incited the crowd:

> *Then they cried out with a loud voice, and stopped their ears, and ran upon him with one accord, and cast him out of the city, and stoned him.*　　　　　　　　Acts 7:57-58

Were these men or beasts? What was stirring them up so? Stephen was drawing the sword of the Spirit

A Compelling Zeal

in and out of their hearts — in and out, in and out. And, oh, it was cutting them! It was cutting them until they could bear it no more. They could have yielded, but they refused to do so. They refused to listen. They screamed, and they stopped their ears. Then they mobbed Stephen, thrust him out of the city and stoned him to death.

These men were so incensed by the audacity of Stephen that they were determined not to stop with him. They were determined to destroy the entire Church of the Lord Jesus Christ.

They soon found a man who wanted to help them. His name was Saul of Tarsus. At first, he was only lightly involved in their plotting. We read:

> *And the witnesses laid down their clothes at a young man's feet, whose name was Saul.*
> Acts 7:58

But Saul became increasingly involved in these anti-Christian activities:

> *And Saul was consenting unto his [Stephen's] death.*
> Acts 8:1

This went on, until finally Saul was obsessed with destroying the Church:

> *He made havoc of the church, entering into every house, and haling men and women committed them to prison.*   Acts 8:3

> *And Saul, yet breathing out threatenings and slaughter against the disciples of the Lord, went unto the high priest, and desired of him letters to Damascus to the synagogues, that if he found any of this way, whether they were men or women, he might bring them bound unto Jerusalem.*   Acts 9:1-2

Paul became a major propagator of this movement, completely absorbed in its desire to erase Christianity from the face of the earth. The movement, which had its roots in Stephen's death, grew and increased long afterwards. Immediately following the account of Stephen's death, we read:

> *And at that time there was a great persecution against the church which was at Jerusalem; and they were all scattered abroad throughout the regions of Judaea and Samaria, except the apostles.*   Acts 8:1

The initial fury of this persecution lasted several years, until the Jews lost one of their greatest leaders — Paul himself. His journey to Damascus

A Compelling Zeal

brought to an end his pillaging of the Church. What happened on the road to Damascus that day caused him to become a pillar of the faith he had so ardently persecuted.

But why did Paul go back to Jerusalem after his conversion? And what happened after he got there? It might have seemed logical for Paul to go back and join the original disciples, but this wasn't the case. He did meet Peter and spent fifteen days with him. He also met James, the Lord's brother, but not any of the other apostles (see Galatians 1:18-19). Paul had gone back to Jerusalem for a much nobler and higher cause. There was something else on his heart, something he felt drawn to, something he felt compelled to do.

Paul did what he could with the apostles during those two short weeks:

> *He was with them coming in and going out at Jerusalem.* Acts 9:28

But the work Paul felt drawn to was another:

> *He spake boldly in the name of the Lord Jesus, and disputed against the Grecians.*
> Acts 9:29

This is what Paul had been waiting for. This is

what he had on his heart to do. He must return to Jerusalem and take up the mantle of Stephen. He must pick up the work where Stephen left off. He went directly to his old cohorts, the bitter persecutors, the angry antagonists, the murderous mob, and began to dispute with them concerning the Lord Jesus Christ. With this, he was challenging the feared Hellenists afresh and anew.

What dedication! What faith! What power! What love! What a compelling zeal! Paul risked his life to give a group of mad persecutors another chance to find Christ and be changed as he had been. Even then, they would not be changed. Their ears were still closed to the truth.

These men didn't hate Stephen. They hated the truth. They had worked with Paul and considered him to be a friend, but now he was speaking the truth. Suddenly, they hated him too. They were feeling that same sword of the Spirit piercing their hearts as it had before. And the result was that they were filled with hate for Paul, as they had been for Stephen. They quickly rose up, as before, and began to plot Paul's death:

They went about to slay him. Acts 9:29

When the believers at Jerusalem knew that the Hellenistic Jews intended to kill Paul as they had

A Compelling Zeal

Stephen, they helped him escape. It wasn't his time to die. He was still a young man, and God needed him. Stephen's time had come, but not Paul's. God could get more glory out of him alive than dead. The Damascus saints had lowered him down in a basket, and now the Jerusalem saints helped him escape on a ship. God had great things in store for this man — and they knew it.

Paul was not shipped off quietly, as some have suggested, because he was lacking in wisdom and power or because he was bothersome and a reproach. These faithful Christians helped him escape because he was a young man with great potential. He had extreme wisdom and power. He was shaking the earth everywhere he went. He was a "ball of fire," a burning flame for God. His compelling zeal moved him to action that produced results.

The fact that the next verse says that the churches had rest did have something to do with Paul, but not in the sense that detractors may have imagined. The other churches did not yet even know Paul. He had not spent any time in either Samaria or Galilee since his conversion. He later wrote:

> *And [I] was unknown by face unto the churches of Judaea which were in Christ: but they had heard only, That he which persecuted us in times past now preacheth the faith*

> *which once he destroyed. And they glorified*
> *God in me.* Galatians 1:22-24

Any of the churches would have been happy to see such an amazing man. Their rest was not a result of being free of Paul. After his escape, however, the Grecians were suddenly quieted. They ceased their mad threatenings and slaughter, and, for the first time since Stephen's death, the noose was loosened from around the disciples' necks. This was the "rest" the Scriptures speak of:

> *Then had the churches rest throughout all Judaea and Galilee, and Samaria, and were edified; and walking in the fear of the Lord, and in the comfort of the Holy Ghost, were multiplied.* Acts 9:31

Most anything we could say about the years Paul spent back in Tarsus would be sheer supposition. We just don't know much about that period. We are not really sure even how long he was there. Various men have guessed at everything from four or five years to fourteen years. We really have no way of knowing for sure.

And what was Paul doing all that time? We don't know. We could suppose that he must "lay low" until the Jews had forgotten about him or thought he

A Compelling Zeal

was dead. He went home to Tarsus and waited until it was God's time for him to come out. A sign may have been agreed upon. Someone would contact him when the time was right. Barnabas was chosen for the job, and when the time was right, he went to Tarsus to seek Paul.

Some would imagine that by the time Barnabas went in search of him, Paul might have lost contact with God and become cold and indifferent. We can only answer this by saying that the Church leadership felt that Paul would be best suited to deal with a situation that had arisen in Antioch (the mixing of Jews and Gentiles in the church there).

> *And when he had found him, he brought him unto Antioch. And it came to pass, that a whole year they assembled themselves with the church, and taught much people. And the disciples were called Christians first in Antioch.* Acts 11:26

What Paul was teaching these believers must have been what they needed. Antioch was not only the first place the people were called Christians, but it also became an important center of evangelism for a large portion of the known world.

All of this goes to prove that having a compelling zeal never hurt anyone. It is always better to have zeal and to make some mistakes than to be safe and do nothing, as so many modern-day Christians have done. The zealous are often misunderstood, and they sometimes rub people the wrong way, but they get things done for God.

Chapter 3

A Recognized Calling

And last of all he was seen of me also, as of one born out of due time. For I am the least of the apostles, that am not meet to be called an apostle, because I persecuted the church of God. But by the grace of God I am what I am: and his grace which was bestowed upon me was not in vain; but I laboured more abundantly than they all: yet not I, but the grace of God which was with me.

1 Corinthians 15:8-10

Paul was not a boastful man, yet he often called himself an apostle (see Romans 1:1 and 11:13, 1 Corinthians 9:1 and 15:9, 2 Corinthians 11:5 and

1 Timothy 2:7). Some scholars have questioned the legitimacy of this claim.

The word *apostle* means "one who is sent," and was used in the New Testament to refer to a person who laid the foundations of the Church. Yet, this word means much more than that. It means "special messenger," and was originally used in reference to a very small group of Jesus' followers. Their witness to the truth of the resurrection made them apostles in a very special sense, and no one today could be an apostle in the same sense as they were apostles. The proof of this is that special thrones are reserved for them in Heaven (see Matthew 19:28 and Luke 22:30).

The resurrection seems to have been the main substance of the "special message" of the original apostles. The importance of the matter lies in Jewish history, so bear with me for a moment as I review the pertinent facts.

Jesus was not the only man who made a claim to the title Christ, "the anointed one." The book of Acts mentions three other men who made that identical claim. Chapter 8, for instance, tells of a man called Simon of Samaria who declared that he *"was some great one"* (Acts 8:9) and confirmed his claims with miracles of a sort — tricks of magic or sorcery. Simon of Samaria was able to convince the people of Samaria that he had extraordinary

A Recognized Calling

powers. Upon seeing his miracles, they responded with the confirmation, *"This man is the great power of God"* (Acts 8:10).

In the fifth chapter of Acts, the great Jewish teacher Gamaliel related the history of two other impersonators of Christ. He told first of a man named Theudas who *"before these days rose up, ... boasting himself to be somebody"* (Acts 5:36). The wording of this phrase is also significant. Theudas was not a mere political leader, patriotic zealot or rabble rouser. He was a false Christ and a very persuasive one, for four hundred men followed him. That is more followers than Jesus had on many occasions. But Theudas *"was slain,"* Gamaliel related, *"and all, as many as obeyed him, were scattered, and brought to nought"* (Acts 5:36).

Gamaliel went on to identify the second man: *"After this man rose up Judas of Galilee in the days of the taxing, and drew away much people after him"* (Acts 5:37). We know the *"days of the taxing"* to be the time of the birth of Jesus. So at the very time of the birth of our Lord, there was another man already proclaiming that he was the Christ of God, that he was the Messiah, the promised King of Israel. Judas *"drew away much people after him."* However, Gamaliel tells us, *"he also perished; and all, even as many as obeyed him, were dispersed"* (Acts 5:37).

In the style of Gamaliel, we might say that after

this there arose one called Jesus of Nazareth. He truly was an amazing man. At the age of twelve He confounded the scholars in the Temple.

There were many rumors concerning His birth. Some thought it was miraculous, while others thought it was illegitimate.

The real work of this man did not begin until He was more than thirty years old. He then began a very wide-ranging teaching ministry and healed the sick. He was quickly recognized as a great teacher. The most learned men of the day came to hear Him speak, and when they did, they were impressed:

> *And all bare him witness, and wondered at the gracious words which proceeded out of his mouth. And they said, Is not this Joseph's son?* Luke 4:22

> *And they were all amazed, and spake among themselves, saying, What a word is this!* Luke 4:36

> *Whence hath this man this wisdom?* Matthew 13:54

The actions of Jesus of Nazareth were just as astonishing as His words:

A Recognized Calling

> *The multitudes marvelled, saying, It was never so in Israel.* Matthew 9:33

> *They were all amazed, ... saying, We never saw it on this fashion.* Mark 2:12

> *Such mighty works are wrought by his hands.* Mark 6:2

> *And they were beyond measure astonished, saying, He hath done all things well.* Mark 7:37

> *And they were all amazed ... saying, We have seen strange things to day.* Luke 5:26

> *Who is this that forgiveth sins also?* Luke 7:49

> *What manner of man is this! for he commandeth even the winds and water, and they obey him.* Luke 8:25

Jesus also made great claims. He said:

> *I am the door of the sheep.* John 10:7

> *I am the bread of life.* John 6:35

I am the light of the world.   John 8:12

I am the way, the truth, and the life.
     John 14:6

I am the resurrection, and the life.
     John 11:25

Great crowds also followed Him. Sometimes He was forced to feed thousands of people through miracles because they had followed Him into a desert place where there was nothing to eat.

When the news of Jesus' healing power spread, people out of all the surrounding cities brought their sick and laid them at His feet. He cast evil spirits out of them and healed *"all that were sick"* (Matthew 8:16). Many sought just to touch the hem of His garment. Even then miracles happened: *"and as many as touched [Him] were made perfectly whole"* (Matthew 14:36).

Jesus also called men to leave their homes and business pursuits and follow Him:

> *Follow me and I will make you fishers of men.*   Matthew 4:19

> *Follow me and let the dead bury their dead.*
>   Matthew 8:22

A Recognized Calling

> *Sell what thou hast and give to the poor ... , come and follow me.*   Matthew 19:21

Thousands did follow Him, but not everyone was convinced that He was who He said He was. Some of them hated Him and sought to do Him harm. One day when Jesus was with some of His disciples in the Garden of Gethsemane, at the foot of the Mount of Olives, a group of men came and took Him captive. They falsely accused Him. They found Him guilty of the false charges they had made against Him. And then they actually crucified Him. His blood ran out, and He *"gave up the ghost."* Then He was taken down from the cross and laid in the borrowed tomb of Joseph of Arimathea nearby.

Jesus of Nazareth had died, as had the false Christs before Him, and all of those who had followed Him were scattered. Would He go down in history as just another imposter?

It was a dark day for Jesus' followers. As far as they were concerned, their leader lay rotting in Joseph's tomb. They had believed Him. They had left their homes, their families and their businesses. They had forsaken all to follow Him. He had promised them that they would never die, and now He Himself was dead. What a terrible development! How difficult to understand and explain!

These disciples had gone out preaching in Jesus'

name. They had even been given power to heal the sick and cast out demons. Now there was no message to preach. They had nothing to testify about. Jesus was dead. There was no name in which to lay hands on the sick. There was no name in which to cast out devils. These men were left hopeless and helpless, the apparent victims of deceit. We can only imagine how they were feeling in those moments.

Three days later, however, something amazing happened. Just as the dawn was beginning to break, the Light of the World was ready to spring forth upon humanity. The ground around Jerusalem began to shake violently. An angel of God descended from Heaven and roiled away the stone which stood at the door of the tomb (see Matthew 28:2). But Jesus of Nazareth, who had said that He was the Christ of God, the Messiah, the Savior of the world, the Deliverer, was not there. He had already come forth from the tomb. He was alive, and He would live forevermore.

What joyous news the disciples received! Jesus was alive! He had fulfilled His claims. He had proven to be the true Christ.

At this point, the work of Jesus on the earth was finished. He had given His life. The Lamb was slain. The blood was shed. The sacrifice was given. He had been wounded, bruised, chastised and striped according to the prediction of Isaiah the prophet

A Recognized Calling

(see Isaiah 53:5). He had conquered sin, death and Hell. He said:

> *It is finished.*   John 19:30

> *Father, ... I have finished the work which thou gavest me to do.*   John 17:1 and 4

The only thing left for Jesus to do now was to ascend into Heaven and send the promised Comforter upon His followers to empower them to be the lights of the world in His stead. And yet, His work was *not* ended, for Jesus remained on the earth for forty more days. During that time He was very active.

That same day Jesus appeared to Mary Magdalene and instructed her to tell the other disciples that she had seen Him. When they heard the news, Peter and John ran to the tomb to see if it was true. Sure enough, Jesus' body was gone. This in itself, however, did not in any way constitute a special message. Where was He? Could they prove that He had risen from the dead? This would not be easy, because some of the Jewish leaders quickly spread a rumor that the disciples had stolen away His body. Their special message must not be simply, "The tomb is empty." It had to be more concrete than that.

They gathered the other disciples into an upper

room that evening. They locked the door for fear of the Jews who were seeking to do them harm. Then suddenly Jesus appeared in their midst — through the locked doors. He showed them His wounded hands, His brow, His feet and His side. He spoke to them, and invited them to touch Him.

Luke, the writer of the Acts of the Apostles, stated in the first chapter that Jesus appeared in this way and showed the disciples *"infallible [never failing, unquestionable] proofs"* as evidence that He was truly alive (Acts 1:3). The disciples needed this assurance. Thomas wasn't the only doubter among them. When Mary Magdalene had run to tell the group that she had seen Jesus, she found that they *"mourned and wept"* (Mark 16:10). When she relayed the glorious news, they simply couldn't believe it (see Mark 16:11). So Jesus appeared for the specific purpose of removing every trace of question, doubt, fear and anxiety from the minds of His followers. Their special message would be, "We have seen the risen Lord! We have heard the voice of the risen Lord! We know that Jesus is alive!" That was powerful.

Jesus was interested in making such an appearance to more than just these ten men. He appeared again eight days later when Thomas was with them. This time, Jesus spoke directly to Thomas. He invited Thomas to put his finger into the nail hole in

A Recognized Calling

His hand. He told Thomas to put his hand into the wound in His side. As a result, Thomas cried out, *"My Lord and my God"* (John 20:28).

That was just the result Jesus had desired. History tells us that Thomas went to the shores of South India to preach the Gospel. If he had gone there and said, "Peter said the tomb is empty," the Indian people might have laughed and said, "Who is this Peter fellow? Where does he live?" If Thomas had proclaimed, "Ten disciples saw the risen Lord," the reply would have been the same. No one would have believed a message like that, for there was no power in it. Thomas must be able to say, "I know that Jesus is alive! I have seen the risen Lord! I touched Him! I heard His voice!" With this message Thomas shook South India in his day and made an impact that lasts until the present time.

Jesus did many other things to prove to His disciples that He was indeed alive:

> *And many other signs truly did Jesus in the presence of his disciples, which are not written in this book.*   John 20:30

This resurrection message apparently became a qualification for apostleship. When choosing a twelfth apostle to take the place of Judas, the disciples decided:

> *Wherefore of these men which have companied with us all the time that the Lord Jesus went in and out among us, ... must one be ordained to be a witness with us of His resurrection.*
>
> Acts 1:22

Now, let us relate all of this to Paul. Since the apostles were men who had seen the risen Lord, how could Paul say that he, too, was an apostle? When Jesus was appearing to these particular disciples during the forty days of His continued stay on earth after the resurrection, Paul was still a zealous Jew. His conversion came some two years later. He could not have seen the Lord in the same way these men and women did. These are the reasons that some scholars put forth for denying the apostleship of Paul.

Paul, however, made his case well. In his first letter to the Corinthians, he reminded his brothers in that city that Christ had died for their sins, that He was buried and that He arose the third day (see 1 Corinthians 15:3-4). Then, he indicated, Jesus was seen by Cephas (another name for Peter) (see 1 Corinthians 15:5). Evidently before Jesus appeared that first night in the Upper Room, He had privately appeared to Simon Peter (see Luke 24:34).

Next, Paul said that Jesus was seen by *"the twelve"* (1 Corinthians 15:5). We know there were only ten

A Recognized Calling

present right then, for Thomas was not there at the time, and Judas had betrayed the Lord and then hanged himself. This term, *"the twelve,"* was quite commonly used to denote the original group of the Lord's disciples (see Matthew 26:20 and 47, Mark 14:10 and 17, Luke 22:14 and 47 and John 6:71 and 20:24). Now, they had seen Him.

But that's not all. Paul went on:

> *After that, he was seen of above five hundred brethren at once.* 1 Corinthians 15:6

During those forty days, Jesus appeared many times and in many places that the gospels and the book of Acts do not tell us about. Sometime and somewhere, there were more than five hundred people gathered together in the Lord's name, and He appeared to them. He also showed them unfailing and unquestionable proof that He was alive.

Still, it doesn't end there:

> *After that, he was seen of James.*
> 1 Corinthians 15:7

James the son of Zebedee and brother of John and James the son of Alphaeus were both part of the twelve. This reference, therefore, is to James the brother of Jesus. Our Lord made a special appearance to His own brother.

Paul went on:

Then he was seen of all the apostles.
                    1 Corinthians 15:7

He had already named more than five hundred people who had seen the Lord after His resurrection, but there were more. Rather than name them all, he just included them all under this heading *"all the apostles."* Jesus was busy during those forty days after His resurrection. He was proving Himself to many people so that they would be able to stand in the days ahead. They could stand if they knew their Lord was alive. (Not all those who saw Jesus became active apostles. More than five hundred were eligible for apostleship, but only a hundred and twenty went into the Upper Room.)

But Paul was not yet finished. He had yet to support his own claims to apostleship. That came next:

And last of all he was seen of me also, as of one born out of due time.
                    1 Corinthians 15:8

So Paul did see the Lord. Jesus made a special appearance to him and proved to him that He was

A Recognized Calling

alive. The Lord made this appearance in a vision on the road to Damascus two years after He had gone back to Heaven. When it happened, Paul was blinded by a great light. The presence of the Lord was so great that he was struck to the ground. And he heard the voice of the Lord speaking to him. His life was never the same after that day, for he, too, had seen the risen Lord. He was an apostle, and he did have a special message.

The Lord was not compelled to appear to Paul. Paul could have gone out preaching: "Peter saw the empty tomb," or "More than five hundred brethren saw the risen Christ," but that was not enough. Such a message would never have stirred the Gentile world. Paul needed his own message. He must be able to say, "I have seen Him! I have touched Him! I heard His voice!"

Like Paul, every one of us needs his own message. We must have our own experience with the Lord. When you tell the people of some non-Christian countries that the Bible says that Jesus is alive, they reply that they have never heard of the Bible, nor of Jesus, nor of you. You must have a personal message. They do not know Peter and Paul. You might just as well be talking about Jack and Jill when it comes to those who are totally unfamiliar with the Bible.

Paul had his own message. He was an apostle. He

had come in contact with the risen Lord. Perhaps a few scattered twenty-first-century scholars can doubt it, but those to whom he ministered never did. When we have a genuine encounter with the living Christ, people will know it.

Far too many people are taking unmerited titles for themselves these days. We have so many self-proclaimed apostles and prophets. What we need is more men and women who have seen the Lord and been touched by Him and to whom He has become a dynamic reality. It is men and women like that who will shake the world in our day.

Chapter 4

A Divine Revelation

For I am the least of the apostles, that am not meet to be called an apostle, because I persecuted the church of God. But by the grace of God I am what I am: and his grace which was bestowed upon me was not in vain; but I laboured more abundantly than they all; yet not I, but the grace of God which was with me.   1 Corinthians 15:9-10

Having established his credentials, Paul continued to speak of his apostleship. In his second letter to the Corinthians he reiterated the same theme:

> *For in nothing am I behind the very chiefest apostles, though I be nothing.*
>
> 2 Corinthians 12:11

Was Paul making a preposterous claim to excellence? Although he was *"as one born out of due time,"* was *"the least of all the apostles,"* and was not even *"worthy to be called an apostle,"* yet he claimed to be used more than others. Who are these others, and particularly the *"they"* of verse 10?

Earlier in 1 Corinthians 15, Paul had named Cephas (Peter), the twelve, more than five hundred brethren, James (the brother of the Lord) and others. Then he said, *"I laboured more abundantly than they all."* So he is saying that he accomplished more than Simon Peter, more than James and John, more than Thomas and more than Barnabas. In fact, he is saying that he accomplished more than any of them and more than *"all"* of them.

Why was it Paul who established the Gentile churches? Why was it upon his shoulders that *"the care of all the churches"* fell (2 Corinthians 11:28)? Why was it that this man was used so mightily by God?

Let us take a closer look at Simon Peter. He was the very first disciple whom Jesus chose, and from that day he held a special place at the Lord's side. Jesus preached from Peter's ship and then gave this

A Divine Revelation

disciple a miraculous harvest of fish to prove His power and authority to him (see Luke 5:3-6).

Jesus healed Peter's mother-in-law (see Matthew 8:14-15, Mark 1:30-31 and Luke 4:39). He encouraged Peter to walk on water with Him (see Matthew 14:29). When He went up to the mountain to be transfigured with Moses and Elijah, He took Peter with Him (see Matthew 17:1-2, Mark 9:2 and Luke 9:28-29).

When Jesus asked the question, *"Whom say ye that I am?"* (Matthew 16:15), it was Peter who answered, *"Thou art the Christ, the Son of the living God"* (Verse 16). Jesus' response was, *"Blessed art thou, Simon Barjona"* (Verse 17) and *"I will give unto thee the keys of the kingdom of heaven"* (Verse 19).

When Jesus needed money to pay His taxes, He sent Peter to catch a fish. In its mouth was a coin of sufficient value to pay for Peter's tax as well (see Matthew 17:27). When Jesus raised Jairus' daughter from death, Peter was there in the room with Him (see Mark 5:37 and Luke 8:51). When Jesus went into the Garden of Gethsemane to pray, He took Peter with Him (see Matthew 26:37 and Mark 14:33). To Peter, Jesus said, *"Satan hath desired to have you, but I have prayed for thee, that thy faith fail not: and when thou art converted, strengthen thy brethren"* (Luke 22:31-32).

Among the disciples, it was Peter who first entered

the empty tomb after Jesus' resurrection (Luke 24:12 and John 20:6). According to the writings of Paul and Luke, Jesus appeared to Peter sometime before He appeared to the other disciples that first night in the Upper Room (Luke 24:34 and 1 Corinthians 15:5). When Jesus appeared on the shores of Gennesaret and gave a second miraculous draught of fish, He later said to Peter, *"Feed my lambs"* (John 21:15), and again, *"Feed my sheep"* (Verse 16).

Peter was the leader of the hundred and twenty who gathered in the Upper Room (see Acts 1:15). After the Holy Ghost came upon them all, it was Peter who was their spokesman (see Acts 2:14). Three thousand souls were saved that day because of his message (see Acts 2:41).

It was Peter who spoke words of healing to a lame man at the Beautiful Gate (see Acts 3:4-6). When thousands of people gathered to see the resulting miracle, it was Peter who preached to them (Verse 12). When the apostles were brought before the high priest for questioning, it was Peter who spoke on their behalf (see Acts 4:8, 13 and 19).

It was Peter who detected the lie of Ananias and Sapphira (see Acts 5:3 and 9). It was his shadow, passing over the sick, that healed those who were laid in the streets where he passed (see Acts 5:15). Because of a miracle done through Peter on behalf of Aeneas, two cities, Lydda and Saron, believed

A Divine Revelation

(see Acts 9:32-35). It was Peter who raised Dorcas to life again in Joppa (see Acts 9:36-40). It was Peter who was chosen first to take the Gospel message to the Gentiles (see Acts 10:5). When Peter was imprisoned, an angel of the Lord appeared to set him free (see Acts 12:7-11).

The Lord gave Peter special preparation by giving him special teaching, showing him special miracles and assigning him special duties. Surely Peter had many more qualifications to be an apostle and to be used by God than Paul did. Peter had walked and talked and eaten and slept with Jesus for more than three years, and Paul was a latecomer to the Gospel.

Although Paul was educated in Jerusalem at the feet of Gamaliel, evidently he had never seen Jesus in the flesh. He was not one of the twelve, nor one of the seventy, nor one of the hundred and twenty. He was not even one of the five hundred. He was not present when Jesus gave His teachings and performed His miracles.

Paul didn't walk on water with Jesus. He didn't help pass out the miraculous loaves and fishes. He was not in the Garden of Gethsemane when Jesus agonized there. Still, it was Paul who excelled in Christian ministry.

When thinking about why some are used more than others, we have always considered as reasons such things as Christian education, background and experience. If we judge this case by these conventional qualifications, then Peter far excelled Paul. There must have been some other reasons.

To me, one of the greatest of these reason is revealed in the case of Peter on the housetop. After he had raised Dorcas to life again in Joppa, he stayed in the city for a while in the house of a man called Simon the Tanner. One day, while Peter was waiting for his hosts to prepare the noonday meal, he went up on the roof to pray. And while he was praying, he fell into a trance.

A vision appeared before Peter. In it, he saw what looked like a sheet sewn together at the four corners to form a basket-like affair. In the basket he saw what he described as *"all manner of fourfooted beasts of the earth, and wild beasts, and creeping things, and fowls of the air"* (Acts 10:12). Then Peter heard a voice saying, *"Rise, Peter; kill and eat"* (Verse 13). He recognized the voice as the Lord's. The command was plain enough. Still, for some reason, Peter answered in the negative.

This is important. Peter heard the voice and knew whose voice it was, but he answered, *"Not so, Lord, for I have never eaten any thing that is common or unclean"* (Verse 14).

The voice spoke again: *"What God hath cleansed, that call not thou common"* (Verse 15). And then the vision faded.

A Divine Revelation

But God had not finished with Peter. The vision appeared a second time. Again Peter saw the basketful of animals. Again the voice came loud and clear. The message was the same — *"Rise, Peter; kill, and eat"* — and again Peter answered negatively.

Then, for the third time, the sheet was seen, and the voice was heard. What was God trying to say to Peter in all of this?

It was time for the Gospel to be taken to the Gentiles, and the Lord had chosen Peter to take the message. He had prepared him especially for this hour, His words and actions through the years having been special grooming for the task at hand. But Peter was clearly reluctant. Again and again the Lord urged Peter by the Holy Spirit to obey, but Peter seemed not to be able to understand. Something prevented him from answering a loud and unmistakable, "Yes, Lord!"

Peter was not simply a rebellious person. His background was hindering him from understanding the revelation God was trying to give him now. It was against sacred Law for him to do what God was bidding, and this didn't make sense to him. It was against what He had been taught from the time he was a child. It was against the thinking of his time. So, for the third time, he answered negatively.

But still God was not finished with him. He spoke to Peter again — this time in a very different way.

Peter had come out of his trance and was wondering what this vision could mean, when he heard the Lord's voice again: *"Behold, three men seek thee. Arise therefore, and get thee down, and go with them, doubting nothing: for I have sent them"* (Acts 10:19-20).

Peter got up and went down to see if someone was indeed standing at the gate, and sure enough, there were some men there waiting. They had been directed by an angel to the very house in which he was staying. This was very unusual.

Peter asked the men some questions about where they wanted to take him and what they would expect of him. They answered him that Cornelius, a centurion stationed in Caesarea, had been directed by an angel to send for him and to hear the message he would bring. When Peter learned that they wanted him to go to the house of a Gentile, he was troubled. The Lord had said, *"Get thee down, and go,"* but Peter was hesitant to obey. Instead, he invited the men to stay the night. This was not technically necessary as it was only midday, but journeys were commonly undertaken early in the morning, so Peter no doubt felt that he was justified in putting off this decision. He was not at all sure that he wanted to go with these men.

It is not difficult to understand Peter's dilemma. If he did go to the home of Gentiles, he knew that he would be in trouble with some of his fellow

A Divine Revelation

believers. They wouldn't understand, just as he was having trouble understanding the Lord's plan. Cornelius was an Italian — definitely a Gentile — and Gentiles were considered unclean. They were even compared to dogs. It was against the Law for Peter to even be found in the presence of a Gentile. He had to have time to think about this, to pray and to decide.

I doubt that Peter slept well that night. I can see him tossing and turning and wrestling with his thoughts. Perhaps he remembered His first experiences with Jesus. Once, he had fished all night long and caught nothing. The next day, Jesus, because the crowds were pressing Him into the sea, asked permission to teach from Peter's boat (see Luke 5:1-3). After teaching the people, Jesus had turned to Peter and said, *"Launch out into the deep, and let down your nets for a draught"* (Luke 5:4). Peter had thought that this was rather odd, because all of his toiling had proven fruitless. He was a very good fisherman, he used good equipment, and fished in the best places. Still, how could he say no to this great teacher? So, out of politeness, he had obeyed.

Perhaps he had not wholeheartedly obeyed on this occasion either. Jesus had said, *"Let down your nets,"* but Peter had let down just one of his nets (see Verse 5). But he could never forget the results! The net he let down was so full of fish that it broke, and it took two boats to carry all the fish. Even then, the two boats were dangerously overloaded (see Verses 6-7).

Perhaps Peter also thought that night of the time he had forsaken Jesus, even after He had risen from the dead. He had taken six of the other disciples and gone fishing (see John 21:2-3). Again they fished all night — employing the best methods, using the best equipment and fishing the best spots — all to no avail (see Verse 3). The next morning Jesus had appeared on the shore and called to them (see Verse 4). When He found that they had nothing to eat, He said, *"Cast the net on the right side of the ship, and ye shall find"* (Verse 6).

Peter had not known right away that it was Jesus. Who was this person who was trying to tell them how to fish? Whoever it was, he had some nerve. Peter was the big fisherman of Galilee. It was probably out of anger, and certainly against his better judgment, that Peter cast the net. But, again, how could he forget the results? He had to call for everyone to help him, and yet they could not pull in the net because of the multitude of fish that they had caught. Peter had felt ashamed of his doubt (see Verse 7).

Now, in Joppa, the Lord was again asking Peter to do something that was definitely against his better judgment. What would happen if he obeyed? And

A Divine Revelation

what would happen if he did not obey? Might there be another miraculous catch of fish?

In the end, Peter decided to obey the Lord and face those who would surely not understand why he had done it. When the morning came, he was ready to go with the men who had been sent to bring him to Caesarea. For added security, however, he asked six other Jews from Joppa to accompany him as witnesses (see Acts 10:23, 45 and 11:12).

When they finally reached the house of Cornelius in Caesarea, a crowd was gathered. Cornelius, his family and his friends were all waiting (see Acts 10:24). Cornelius once more explained how he had been directed by an angel to call for Peter in the first place (Acts 10:30-33).

Then, the introductions ended, Peter began to preach (see Verse 34). The message he brought that day was one that he had never preached before, and as he was preaching that message, something happened that had never happened before. Even before he finished the message, the Holy Spirit fell on all the people who had gathered in Cornelius' house (see Verse 44).

This was very unusual. Prior to this time, the Holy Ghost had been given only to the Jews and only through the laying on of hands. These were not Jews, and no one had laid hands on them. God had given Peter a new message, and now He was doing, through Peter, a new thing. It was for this day that the Lord had prepared him.

Did Peter learn his lesson well? He said that the Lord had shown him *"that [he] should not call any man common or unclean"* (Acts 10:28), *"that God is no respecter of persons"* (Verse 34), that *"in every nation he that feareth him, and worketh righteousness, is accepted with him"* (Verse 35), and that *"he is Lord of all"* (Verse 36). In keeping with this revelation, Peter continued to minister to the Gentiles, until ...

Some years later, Peter was again ministering to Gentiles. When he learned that some of the disciples of James would be coming to that place, he decided to separate himself from the Gentiles, fearing the reaction of the co-workers of the Lord's brother (see Galatians 2:12). Paul later wrote, *"When Peter was come to Antioch, I withstood him to the face, because he was to be blamed"* (Verse 11).

This is amazing. Paul, who was *"the least of the apostles,"* and who was *"not worthy to be called an apostle,"* felt compelled to confront the apostle Peter with what he considered to be a serious breach of conduct. Only a divine revelation could give a man courage and determination to do a thing like that, and I believe this is the reason Paul was so mightily used by God!

Another man who had great opportunities to be used of the Lord was Joses, a Levite of Cyprus. The

A Divine Revelation

disciples called him *"Barnabas"* (Acts 4:36). Whether or not Barnabas was one of the five hundred or one of the hundred and twenty we cannot say for sure. We can say that we hear of Barnabas long before we hear of Paul.

Barnabas was among the first disciples who sold their land and gave the money derived from the sale for the propagation of their new faith (see Acts 4:37). He had been in the Christian realm longer and, therefore, had a better background, better understanding of Christian teachings, and more experience than did Paul.

At first, Paul had not been well received by the early Church leaders. When he was forced to leave Damascus, he tried to join himself to the apostles at Jerusalem, but they were hesitant to receive him because of his past participation in the persecution. Barnabas showed great wisdom on this occasion:

> *But Barnabas took him, and brought him to the apostles, and declared unto them how he had seen the Lord in the way, and that he had spoken to him, and how he had preached boldly at Damascus in the name of Jesus.*
> Acts 9:27

Because the Church leaders respected the opinion

of Barnabas, they received Paul — on the basis of that recommendation.

Later, Barnabas was chosen by the leadership of the Church as the best man to deal with the very difficult situation that had arisen in Antioch. He, in turn, brought Paul into the picture. The united efforts of these two men produced in Antioch a dynamic congregation in which believers were so Christ-like that they were called *"Christians"* (Acts 11:26).

The congregation at Antioch was blessed with prophets and teachers. One day, while this group of mature believers was praying, the Spirit spoke to them:

> *Separate me Barnabas and Saul for the work whereunto I have called them.*   Acts 13:2

These two men were chosen for the missionary ministry at exactly the same time. Then, having fasted and prayed, the church leaders laid hands on them both and sent them out together. They were apparently on equal footing.

From the very first, however, it seems that Paul stood out as the leader of this new missionary ministry. From that point on, we find recorded only Paul's messages and only Paul's miracles.

A Divine Revelation

Barnabas was mentioned only occasionally in the biblical account.

It was Paul who rebuked Elymas the sorcerer and brought the curse of blindness upon him, causing the deputy, Sergius Paulus, to believe (see Acts 13:6-12). It was Paul who preached in Antioch in Pisidia, winning many Gentiles to the faith (Acts 13:14-49). It was Paul who spoke the words of healing to the impotent cripple at Lystra (Acts 14:8-10). An interesting reaction was produced in the people of that place:

> *And when the people saw what Paul had done, they lifted up their voices, saying in the speech of Lycaonia, The gods are come down to us in the likeness of men.* Acts 14:11

The people of Lystra gave Paul and Barnabas names after their own gods. They called Paul *"Mercurius [Mercury]"* because he was the chief spokesman (Acts 14:12). Mercury was the Roman messenger god, known to the Greeks as "Hermes." And what did they call Barnabas?

> *They called Barnabas, Jupiter.* Acts 14:12

This is astonishing. Jupiter was the king of all the gods, the chief god, the master of them all, the very father of the gods. The people of Lystra saw something compelling in the personal appearance and commanding character of Barnabas, and consequently they called him Jupiter, the god the Greeks knew as "Zeus." The priest of Jupiter proceeded to bring oxen and garlands and was about to lead the people in sacrifice (see Verse 13). Barnabas was an impressive man.

The two men finished their first missionary journey and went "home" to Antioch. They stayed there for some time, teaching and preaching the Word of the Lord, but eventually the Spirit spoke to Paul that it was time for them to go again.

Paul suggested to Barnabas that they visit the newly-formed churches to strengthen the new believers in the faith. Barnabas was willing to go, but he wanted to take along his cousin, John Mark. Paul couldn't agree with this. They had taken John Mark once before, and he had left them in Pamphylia. In this way, a sharp contention developed between the two men:

> *And the contention was so sharp between them, that they departed asunder one from the other: and so Barnabas took Mark, and sailed unto Cyprus.* Acts 15:39

Was this just a personal difference? Was it just a clash of personalities? Or was it something much

A Divine Revelation

more serious, a question of right and wrong, for example? Was it the Lord's will for them to take Mark with them? Or was it not the Lord's will to take him?

What was going on here? Was one of these men right and the other one wrong? Did one of them have the Spirit's leading and the other one have his own plan? Was one of them obeying God's plan and one of them rebelling against that plan?

Barnabas, whether he was right or wrong, took Mark, and they set off on their missionary journey. Paul, whether he was right or wrong, now selected Silas as his new companion, and the two of them set off on a different journey.

From that moment on, nothing more is written of Barnabas and Mark in the biblical record, but chapter after chapter is written of the works of Christ through Paul and his several companions through the years. In fact, the entire balance of thirteen chapters of the written history of the early Church is devoted to the life of Paul.

John Mark was a fine young man with possibilities that Barnabas recognized and desired to encourage. Indeed, John Mark would later be used by the Lord to write the gospel of Mark. At that moment, however, he was still unstable in Paul's view. The intentions of Barnabas to give the lad another chance were very noble. What a shame that the matter had to divide two such powerful ministry companions!

But there is more. Barnabas was also involved in the Gentile question. Immediately following the verses concerning Peter's separating himself from the Gentiles, we read:

> *And the other Jews dissembled likewise with him; insomuch that Barnabas also was carried away with their dissimulation.*
>
> Galatians 2:13

It apparently took a lot of pressure to move Barnabas, but he was eventually moved, "carried away."

The Bible has much good to say of Barnabas, particularly that *"he was a good man, full of the Holy Ghost and of faith"* (Acts 11:24). Perhaps if he had remained with Paul, he could have continued to take a bold stand against legalistic Jews on issues of Law. It takes a divine revelation to stand against the majority. I believe this is the reason Paul could say that he was *"used more abundantly."*

There were other disciples with amazing potential. John, for instance, was called *"the disciple whom Jesus loved,"* and he *"leaned on his [Jesus'] breast"* (John 21:20). He saw the miraculous draught of fish (Luke 5:7 and 10). He was there to see Moses and Elijah

A Divine Revelation

on the Mount of Transfiguration (Matthew 17:1-3) and to see the dead girl raised to life again (Mark 5:37). He was in the Upper Room and the garden of Gethsemane (see Mark 14). He saw Jesus calm the storm (see Luke 8) and heard the Sermon on the Mount (Matthew 5-7). He wrote the book of John, the three letters to the churches that bear his name, and the book of Revelation.

James, too, was in the inner circle (Matthew 17:1). He died a martyr for Christ (Acts 12:2). And what about Thomas? The Lord made a special appearance to him in the Upper Room (John 20:24-29).

What about Matthew? He wrote a biography of Jesus. What about Andrew? Philip? Bartholomew? James the son of Alphaeus? Thaddaeus? Simon the Canaanite? Why was Paul used more abundantly than all of them? Little else is mentioned in the Scriptures about any one of these. Why? Is it possible that some of them were among *"the Jews"* that were drawn aside with Peter and Barnabas? We cannot be sure. But Paul did have more to say on this subject.

Continuing his narrative of the second chapter of Galatians, Paul related the outcome of some discussions he had with Church leaders in Jerusalem. He was concerned about certain brothers, whom he went so far as to call *"false"* (Verse 4), who had arrived in Galatia to try to force Jewish Law on the newly converted Gentiles. Paul felt that the Law was a *"yoke of bondage"* (Galatians 5:1). Determined that truth, not tradition, would prevail in the works he had established, he decided not to give these men opportunity to minister (see Galatians 2:5). He realized that this could be misinterpreted and that if he developed an open rift with Jerusalem, it could do irreparable damage to his ministry. He wrote:

> *And I went up by revelation and communicated unto them that gospel which I preach among the Gentiles, but privately to them which were of reputation, lest by any means I should run, or had run, in vain.*
>
> Galatians 2:2

Whatever Paul's reasons for going to Jerusalem, this private meeting with Church leaders was extremely important to the further development of the Gospel. The meeting was strained, however, complicated by the fact that Paul had refused to insist that Titus be circumcised (see Galatians 2:3).

Paul's reflections on the outcome of this meeting seem to be particularly harsh. He wrote:

> *But of these who seemed to be somewhat, (whatsoever they were, it maketh no matter to me: God accepteth no man's person:) for*

A Divine Revelation

> *they who seemed to be somewhat in conference added nothing to me: but contrariwise ... .*
> Galatians 2:6-7

Twice in one sentence Paul said that these men *"seemed to be somewhat."* Yet he contends, *"[They] added nothing to me: but contrariwise... ."* He meant that just the opposite was true. Rather than the men having something to teach him, he had something to share with them.

I know that this doesn't seem to make sense, and we all wonder how it could be possible. What I know is that some men know what they have seen and heard, while others (Paul among them) have received *"the revelation of Jesus Christ."*

Who were these men to whom Paul is referring here? He named three of them in verse 9, and they were none other than James, Cephas (Peter) and John. This James could not have been the original disciple named James because he had already been beheaded by Herod. The other two, however, were part of what we commonly know as "the inner circle" of disciples. They were in the Upper Room on the Day of Pentecost and heard the sound of the rushing mighty wind. The cloven tongues of fire that appeared that day sat upon their heads, and they were filled with the Holy Ghost. They also spoke with other tongues as the Spirit gave them utterance. Still, they struggled to lay aside tradition, teaching, ritual and pattern and be led by the Holy Spirit.

This should not surprise us. We are always trying to move mountains with might and power, when God said it could only be done by His Spirit. We try to conquer Jericho with spears and swords, but the walls of that city will never fall that way. We try to build a bridge across the Red Sea, but the enemy overtakes us while we are in the process. We try to gather a week's supply of manna, and then we are surprised when it all spoils before the next day.

On this occasion mentioned by Paul in Antioch, when Peter, Barnabas and others abandoned the Gentile ministry for fear of criticism from others, Paul again had some very harsh things to say about them:

> *But when I saw that they walked not uprightly according to the truth of the gospel, I said unto Peter before them all ... .*
>
> Galatians 2:14

Paul was so offended by the attitude of these brothers, considering it to be totally inconsistent with the message of Christ, that he began preaching to them. The rest of the verses of this chapter

A Divine Revelation

were spoken, not to heathen Gentiles but to fellow Church leaders.

What was this terrible struggle that was plaguing the early Church? Was it a racial problem? Was it a religious issue?

Jesus was a Jew and had taught His Jewish disciples the Jewish Law. He had told them, *"Go not into the way of the Gentiles, ... but go rather to the lost sheep of the house of Israel"* (Matthew 10:5). They had seen Him teaching in the Jewish synagogues (Matthew 4:23, 9:35, Mark 1:39 and Luke 4:15 and 44). And they had heard Him call the Gentiles *"dogs"* (Matthew 15:26 and Mark 7:27).

The conversion of the Gentiles, however, had been prophesied down through the ages (see, for instance, Genesis 22:18, Psalm 22:27, 86:9, Isaiah 9:2, 49:6, 60:3, Daniel 7:14 and Hosea 2:23). Jesus Himself had gone to a Gentile area (see Matthew 15:21) and had ministered to a Gentile woman, lauding her *"great faith"* (Matthew 15:22-28). He had offered to go to the home of a centurion to heal his servant (see Matthew 8:7). When that man recognized Christ's authority to heal by speaking the word at a distance, Jesus had commended him by saying, *"I have not found so great faith, no, not in Israel"* (Matthew 8:10).

When giving the disciples the plan of world evangelization, Jesus made it clear that the Gentiles were to have all the benefits of the Gospel:

> *Go ye therefore, and teach ALL NATIONS.*
> Matthew 28:19

> *Go ye into ALL THE WORLD, and preach the gospel TO EVERY CREATURE.*
> Mark 16:15

> *And ye shall be witnesses unto me both in Jerusalem, and in all Judaea, and in Samaria, and UNTO THE UTTERMOST PART OF THE EARTH.*
> Acts 1:8

Still, the transition from Law to grace for these disciples was a difficult one, largely because their Jewish traditions had been so deeply in grained in them through years of study and religious practice. So maybe they can be excused.

But wait a minute! Wasn't Paul a Jew too? He was a Pharisee (see Philippians 3:5) and the son of a Pharisee (see Acts 23:6). He was also *"of the tribe of Benjamin"* (Romans 11:1). Peter wasn't a Pharisee. John wasn't a Pharisee. Barnabas was a Levite (see Acts 4:36), but not a Pharisee. Paul was a member of the strictest religious order (see Acts 26:5). In fact, he said, *"[I] profited in the Jews' religion above*

A Divine Revelation

many my equals in mine own nation, being more exceedingly zealous of the traditions of my fathers" (Galatians 1:14).

Paul was as deeply rooted in Judaism or even more so than the rest of them. Peter had been a fisherman while Paul was being a trained as a religious leader. Paul was *"exceedingly zealous of the traditions."* Still, when he met the Lord Jesus Christ, he threw away his tradition, his background, his teachings and his rituals, got on his knees and began to wait before God for a revelation of divine truth.

This knee exercise became a common thing in Paul's life. It gave him power to do special miracles. It gave him wisdom to reveal the mysteries of the Gospel. It gave him authority to rebuke those who strayed from the truth. It gave him courage to face persecution. It gave him grace to fight a good fight, finish the course and keep the faith.

Many of the letters of Paul contain rebuke. To the Corinthians he said:

> *For it hath been declared unto me of you, my brethren, by them which are of the house of Chloe, that there are contentions among you.*
> 1 Corinthians 1:11

> *I told you before, and foretell you, as if I were present, the second time; and being absent*

> *now I write to them which heretofore have sinned, and to all other, that, if I come again, I will not spare.* 2 Corinthians 13:2

To the Galatians Paul wrote:

> *I marvel that you are so soon removed from him that called you into the grace of Christ unto another gospel.* Galatians 1:6

But who wrote Paul letters of rebuke? Who withstood him to the face? Who felt the need to preach to him? Who said, "Paul, I marvel that you are so soon removed from the Gospel of Christ"? I am convinced that Paul excelled because he lived by divine revelation.

Paul spoke by revelation:

> *For I have received of the Lord that which also I delivered unto you.*
> 1 Corinthians 11:23

Paul walked by revelation:

> *And I went up by revelation and communicated unto them that gospel which I preach among the Gentiles.* Galatians 2:2

A Divine Revelation

If we desire to be used by the Lord, we must become willing to wait on our knees for a divine revelation and then to obey that revelation — whatever the cost.

Chapter 5

A Total Commitment

For I will shew him how great things he must suffer for my name's sake.   Acts 9:16

But none of these things move me, neither count I my life dear unto myself, so that I might finish my course with joy, and the ministry, which I have received of the Lord Jesus, to testify the gospel of the grace of God.
                                             Acts 20:24

Many things work together to make a great man or woman of God. It is not always easy to point to any single character trait, to any single revelation or to any single experience and say, "That it is the key to successful Christian living." Effectiveness in the Christian life depends on a combination of many important character traits, many great revelations and many great experiences. The depth and magnitude of our Christian character, our revelations from God and our experiences in the walk of faith largely determine how effective we can be as persons and as ministers.

At least one experience in Paul's life seems to be unique in Bible history. This experience apparently did something very special for him that helped him to attain his recognized position as the chief of apostles.

It happened only a few days after Paul was converted. He had not yet preached any sermons. In fact, he hadn't even testified. He had not established a single church. He had not yet received any knowledge of the *"mysteries of the kingdom."* He was newly converted — a babe in Christ.

While he was on his way to Damascus that day to persecute the Christians there, a great light had suddenly enveloped him, he had been struck to the ground by an unseen force, and the Lord had spoken to him (see Acts 9:3-7). He was then led blind into Damascus, and for the next three days he neither ate nor drank anything (Verses 8-9). The Lord had commanded him, *"Arise, and go into*

A Total Commitment

the city, and it shall be told thee what thou must do" (Verse 6).

Three days later, while Paul was praying, the Lord spoke to Ananias, a disciple of that city (Verse 10). Through a vision, he was instructed to go to Straight Street to the house of a man named Judas, where he was to find Paul praying (see Verse 11). Meanwhile, Paul also had received a vision in which he saw a man named Ananias coming into the room and laying his hands on him. As Ananias did this, Paul's sight returned (see Verse 12).

Ananias wasn't immediately willing to obey his heavenly vision because he had heard of Saul of Tarsus and his persecution of the Church, and so he feared him (see Verses 13-14). The Lord calmed his fears:

> *But the Lord said unto him, Go thy way: for he is a chosen vessel unto me, to bear my name before the Gentiles, and kings, and the children of Israel: for I will shew him how great things he must suffer for my name's sake.* Acts 9:15-16

I find these words, *"I will shew him how great things he must suffer for my name's sake,"* to be astonishing. Bear with me for a moment as I attempt to make a balanced presentation of this very important and misunderstood subject. There are two sides to this coin, as we shall see.

What was happening here? Before Paul would make a single move for Christ, a special revelation must come to him. Before he attempted in any way to exalt the name of Jesus, the Lord must speak to him. Before he preached one sermon, before he prayed for any sick, before he cast out any demons, before he won a single soul, he must know the price he would be called upon to pay.

This revelation that Paul was about to receive was not a revelation of doctrinal truth. It was not a revelation of mystery. It was not a revelation of power. It was not a revelation of victory. It was not a revelation of prosperity. It was, of all things, a revelation of suffering. God said, *"For I will shew him how great things he must suffer for my name's sake."*

We don't know exactly how this revelation came to Paul. The Bible doesn't say. Perhaps it came in a vision. Perhaps Paul had a spiritual dream. Perhaps he heard the audible voice of the Lord. Or perhaps the Lord spoke these words of revelation through Ananias. However it came, we know that the Lord did speak to Paul this strange message, and although we don't know the exact words of the message, we do know the content of the message. We can roughly reconstruct the message from the information we

A Total Commitment

find recorded in the writings of Luke and of Paul himself. It would go something like this:

> *Paul, My son, if you choose to follow Me, you will suffer. I want you to know that. You will be a partaker of My sufferings. You will suffer with Me.*
>
> *You have been a zealous Jew. You prospered in the Jews' religion, but now the Jews will hate you. Your own people will reject you. They will persecute you and even try to kill you. When they find you preaching in My name, they will beat you with thirty-nine stripes, according to the full measure of the Law. This will not happen just once. The Jews will beat you in this way five different times.*
>
> *If you follow Me, son, I will send you to preach in Philipi. You will cast the demon out of a woman possessed with a spirit of divination. Because of this, her masters will be angry and will capture you. They will bring you before the magistrate. A large mob will protest against you. The magistrate will rip off your clothes in the sight of all the people. They will lay you face down upon the ground and, at the magistrate's command, will beat you with a rod. In your lifetime you will be beaten in this way at least three times.*

In Philipi they will thrust you into the inner prison and put your feet in stocks. You will be imprisoned many times.

I will send you to preach in Lystra. Certain Jews will come out of the cities of Antioch and Iconium and will stir up the people against you. They will stone you until they think you are dead. Then they will drag you outside the city and leave you, but your suffering will not end there. I will have more work for you to do.

When you go back to Jerusalem, where you were raised at the feet of Gamaliel, the Jews of Asia will stir up the people against you. While some are beating you, others will be plotting your death. Soldiers will save you from their plans, but will bind you with two chains. They will be forced to carry you away bodily to prevent any further mob violence. The next day they will present you before the council. When you try to defend yourself, they will slap you. Such a division will arise among the council that the soldiers will have to rescue you or the angry mob would pull you apart.

The following day more than forty Jews will bind themselves together under a curse, determined that they will not eat or drink until they see you dead.

A Total Commitment

The chief captain will be forced to send you to Caesarea to Felix, the governor. It will take two hundred soldiers, seventy horsemen and two hundred spearmen to protect you from the angry mobs. Even then, you will have to travel in the safety of night. They will keep you in Herod's judgment hall until witnesses come to testify against you.

Five days later, the high priest Ananias will come with the elders and an orator named Tertulus. Tertulus will accuse you of being a pestilent fellow, a mover of sedition among all the Jews throughout the world, a ringleader of the sect of the Nazarenes and one who has profaned the Temple. When he has finished speaking, all the Jews present will agree that these things are true, but will be unable to prove them. However, Felix will continue to hold you to please them.

The Jews, thinking that you will come back to Jerusalem, will lie in wait to kill you. When you fail to arrive, they will come to Caesarea about ten days later to appear as witnesses against you before Porcius Festus. They will make many grievous complaints against you, but again will not be able to prove them.

Later, they will bring you before Agrippa. As you are making your defense, Festus will accuse you of being mad, but Agrippa will find nothing against you.

You will be sent to Rome to appear before Caesar Augustus himself. On the way to Rome, your ship will be wrecked. You will suffer shipwreck three times. On one of these occasions, there will be no way of rescue, and you will spend all night and all day in the deep water.

In Rome you will be a captive in your own house for more than two years. You may welcome the rest, for from this day until the day you die, you will be in constant journeyings.

With these journeys will come perils. Many perils await you. Whether you are in the city or in the wilderness, whether you are on the land or on the sea, grievous perils await. Robbers will molest you, and false brethren will equally molest you.

Paul, with the journeys and the perils will come constant weariness. There will be painfulness. At times you will be hungry, and there will be times of great thirst. You will be called upon to fast often. There will be times of extreme cold. At times you will not have sufficient clothing.

Your hardships will begin very shortly, for the governor under Aretas, the Arabian king,

A Total Commitment

will send a garrison to this city in an attempt to capture you. You will have to flee, being let down in a basket from a window on the wall.

But, My son, these are just physical sufferings. The cross you will carry will be much heavier. The night you face will be much darker. The road you walk will be much rougher. For you must bend your back, and I will place upon your shoulders the care of all the churches. You will never be able to cast off this burden.

That, in substance, was the revelation that came to Paul: *"For I will shew him how great things he must suffer for my name's sake."* To Paul, who was three days old in Christ, that was the revelation: suffering, hardship, bondage, persecution — a heavy cross, a dark night, a rough road. That was the substance of God's special message to Paul: shame, reproach, being herded around with filthy prisoners, being despised, rejected, misunderstood, losing everything that men hold dear.

There is always a price to pay for excellence — whether it be in earthly matters or the spiritual. Just as we could say that not many men have been used in the same measure as was Paul, we would also have to say that not many have been willing to pay the price he paid. God placed a price tag on

Paul's ministry, then waited to see if he was willing to pay the price. And he was.

While I still a very young minister, I was conducting a series of meetings in a church in Pittsburgh, Pennsylvania. Each evening many people would stand and testify to what the Lord had done for them. Usually, each testimony began in a similar way: "I love the Lord tonight because ..." After this had gone on for several evenings, one night the Lord spoke to all of us in prophecy through a young lady. He said, "Ye say that ye love Me, but how much do you love Me? Do you love Me enough to carry My message to the lost and dying — the multitudes in the valley of despair?"

In that moment, I stood in awe at the presence of God, and could not bring myself to speak for the longest time. Those words echoed over and over in my spirit. "How much do you love? How much do you love Me?"

"Do you love Me enough? Do you love Me enough? Do you love Me enough?"

The Lord was saying, "Are you willing to pay the price? Are you willing to pay the price? Are you willing to pay the price?"

And this is exactly what the Lord was asking Paul. "How much do you love Me, Paul? Do you love Me enough to pay the price?"

If the revelation came in a dream or a vision,

A Total Commitment

Paul had seen himself lying naked in the dust while angry mobs beat him with rods. He had seen his blood shed at least nine times. He had seen himself struggling for life in the water. It is even possible that he envisaged his own head tumbling off in Rome. We cannot be sure.

Although the Bible says nothing of the actual death of Paul, other historical sources do. The historian Tacitus, in the fifteenth book of his *Annals,* described a great persecution of Christians in the year AD 64. Other sources confirm the deaths of both Peter and Paul in that same period.

Peter was described by Tertullian, in AD 200, as having died as his Lord died — crucified upside down during the great persecution under the Roman emperor Nero. Paul, it is stated, died as did John the Baptist, giving his head for the sake of the Gospel.

Clement, bishop of Rome (AD 88-97), in his letter to Corinth (AD 95), Eusebius in his *Church History* published in AD 326, Caius (AD 283-296) and Dionysius, Bishop of Corinth (AD 169-174), all confirmed the beheading of Paul in Rome, evidently in AD 64, but perhaps as late as AD 67.

Maybe Paul knew it from the first day. And now the Lord was asking him, "Are you willing? Will you pay the price? Do you love Me enough?" What a powerful moment of decision!

What percentage of our modern Christians have shed their blood even once for the sake of Christ? Have most of us taken even ten stripes for His sake or had even a few stones thrown at us? And yet, far too many of our modern believers have turned back because of "hardship and persecution." Each of us knows hundreds and even thousands who have either turned back or, at the very least, become inactive in the face of "hardship" — when actually we don't even know what hardship is! Most of us have not yet faced real persecution.

Paul was about to enter a life of suffering and hardship, and it had all been made clear to him. Still, he did not waver or turn back. He had made a total commitment. He said, "Yes, Lord," and went forward.

Paul was a man who could face hardship with a song in his heart. I am reminded of the wonderful hymn by Jack and Billy Campbell:

Jesus, Use Me

Dear Lord, I'll be a witness,
If You will help my weakness.
I know that I'm not worthy, Lord, of Thee.
By eyes of faith I see Thee
Upon the cross of Calvary.
Dear Lord, I cry, let me Thy servant be.

A Total Commitment

I'll stand by Thee, dear Jesus,
Till death shall come my way.
I'll spread the Gospel to the fallen here.
And, if it be Thy will, Lord,
To go across the sea,
Help me, Lord, to be willing to say "Yes."

He's the Lily of the Valley,
The Bright and Morning Star.
He's the Fairest of Ten Thousand
To my soul.
He's the beautiful Rose of Sharon.
He's all the world to me.
But, best of all, He is my coming King.

Chorus:

Jesus, use me!
And, oh, Lord, don't refuse me,
For surely there's a work that I can do.
And, even though it's humble,
Lord, cause my will to crumble.
Though the cost be great, I'll work for You.

Somehow I think that Paul would have added to the final line:

And though the valley be deep,
I'll work for You.

*And though the journey be long,
I'll work for You.
And though the way be rough,
I'll work for You.
And though the shadows be dark,
I'll work for You.
And though the mountains be steep,
I'll work for You.
And though it cost my life,
I'll work for You.*

Paul was not well founded in Christian doctrine as yet. He could not have had on the whole armor of God yet. So what then enabled him to make such a total commitment? For one thing, he had experienced a genuine conversion.

Paul's experience on the road to Damascus was real. This was not a momentary response to an emotional altar call. This was not a passing New Year's resolution. This was not a mere turning over of a new leaf. This man met the Master. He caught a glimpse of the Savior's face, and his life was forever changed. Old things passed away, and all things became new.

Suddenly, the murder was gone from his heart, and the blasphemy was gone. He no longer felt like being troublesome to the Church, but now

A Total Commitment

desired to further the Gospel which he had once opposed.

This was not just a story Paul had learned in Sunday school class. This was real. He felt it. And because his life had been changed, he loved Jesus (whom he had just met) and he loved Jesus enough to do His bidding. Beyond his genuine conversion, he had a compelling zeal and a well-defined calling, and this enabled him to make a total commitment.

God has not changed. He is calling every one of us to make a commitment to Him. Let us tell Him:

Lord, I will carry the heaviest cross on the roughest road through the darkest night.

Paul foresaw what he would face, but he was ready to face anything. He later had another, similar experience:

And now, behold, I go bound in the Spirit unto Jerusalem, not knowing the things that shall befall me there: save that the Holy Ghost witnesseth in every city, saying that bonds and afflictions abide [await] me.
Acts 20:22-23

On his final trip to Jerusalem, Paul was continually reminded by the Holy Spirit in every city that suffering lay ahead. He did not always know the form the persecution would take, but he did know that *"bonds and afflictions"* awaited him. The disciples of Tyre warned him. Luke warned him. Phillip and his daughters warned him. And the prophet Agabus warned him. We will discuss these cases more fully in the next chapter.

The other modes of revelation through which Paul received this message are not mentioned in the Scriptures. Possibly this message came through dreams or visions or through an audible voice. Possibly it came as prophecy or interpretation of tongues in the various assemblies. Maybe it came in various ways in the different cities. But, however they came, the messages all agreed — ROUGH ROAD AHEAD! Still, Paul refused to take any detours. He said:

> *But none of these things move me, neither count I my life dear unto myself, so that I might finish my course with joy, and the ministry, which I have received of the lord Jesus, to testify the gospel of the grace of God.*
> Acts 20:24

"None of these things move me!" Paul was ready to give his life. He was concerned with just one thing — *"the ministry."* He was glad to suffer if others could know the Lord Jesus Christ through his suffering.

A Total Commitment

Paul did not matter, but lost and dying souls did. He was ready to give himself as the alabaster box of ointment, to be broken, so that the sweet fragrance might flow out and minister to others, and thus to Christ.

Paul willingly gave himself to be beaten, to be stoned, to be hated, to be mocked, to be misunderstood, to be slapped, to be arrested, to be chained, to be robbed, to be molested — and if necessary, to be killed.

I know men who have been beaten for Christ. I know men who have been arrested for Christ. I know men who have been called mad for Christ. I know men who have been hated and rejected for Christ. But I don't know any one man who has had the abundance of afflictions that Paul bore for the precious name of the Lord Jesus. This is the reason that the attitude that Paul took toward such matters is very important to us. Very early in his Christian life he developed the proper attitude toward suffering and the Christian faith.

For one thing, Paul did not use these things as a source of boasting. If any man had the right to boast of hardship and persecution, Paul did. If any man ever had the right to tell others what he had endured for the Gospel, he had that right. But Paul did not make a practice of enumerating or even mentioning these afflictions. It is only in his second letter to the Corinthians that we find them recorded in detail (see 2 Corinthians 11:24-28).

Why did Paul break his precedent in this case and pour out his burden upon the Corinthians? What was it that he said to them? He said there were certain false brethren who were boasting of their achievements and their sufferings for the Lord:

> *Seeing that many glory after the flesh, I will glory also.* 2 Corinthians 11:18

> *Are they ministers of Christ? (I speak as a fool) I am more; in labours more abundantly, in stripes above measure, in prisons more frequent, in deaths oft.* 2 Corinthians 11:23

Before he began this list of sufferings, Paul stated, *"I speak foolishly"* (Verse 21), *"I speak as a fool"* (Verse 23). Only then did he talk about persecutions and hardships. This shows us that it would be foolish to boast of these things.

Many years ago I overheard a missionary addressing a large Christian convention in South India. "They threw rotten tomatoes and eggs at me in the north," he lamented. This "persecution" had made him go south — where the going was not so "rough." It was obvious that everyone thought of that man

A Total Commitment

as a fool, and according to Paul's teachings, he was just that. Tomatoes and rotten eggs! Most of us in the West have no idea what real persecution looks like. Most of us have never looked into the face of genuine hardship.

I would like to have an actual count of people over the past few years who have said, "Brother, I would like to work for the Lord, but I'm so poor, and I have such a large family, and my education is limited, and people are against me," and on and on it goes. We have many fools in the Christian ranks. Our troops seem to be made up of grumblers and complainers.

To the Romans Paul wrote:

> *For I reckon that the sufferings of this present time are not worthy to be compared with the glory which shall be revealed in us.*
>
> Romans 8:18

Our sufferings are not even worth mentioning. Forget about them. Stop making excuses. Make those stumbling blocks into stepping stones.

To the Galatians Paul wrote:

> *God forbid that I should glory, save in the cross of our Lord Jesus Christ.*
>
> Galatians 6:14

To the Ephesians He said:

> *Giving thanks always for all things unto God and the Father in the name of our Lord Jesus Christ ...* Ephesians 5:20

To the Philippians he said:

> *I can do all things through Christ which strengtheneth me.* Philippians 4:13

To the Colossians he said:

> *[I] now rejoice in my sufferings for you.*
> Colossians 1:24

To the Thessalonians he said:

> *In every thing give thanks: for this is the will of God in Christ Jesus concerning you.*
> 1 Thessalonians 5:18

Paul enumerated his sufferings only to the Corinthians, and only to show them how foolish it was to boast in this way. He did speak of his sufferings when writing to Timothy. In this case, he did not list them, as he had to the Corinthians, but simply

A Total Commitment

mentioned them and used them to teach young Timothy what he would face, so that he could prepare. Notice that suffering was presented in a very positive way:

> *For God hath not given us the spirit of fear; but of power, and of love, and of a sound mind. Be not thou therefore ashamed of the testimony of our Lord, nor of me his prisoner: but be thou partaker of the afflictions of the gospel according to the power of God.*
> 2 Timothy 1:7-8

> *For the which cause I also suffer these things: nevertheless, I am not ashamed: for I know whom I have believed, and am persuaded that he is able to keep that which I have committed unto him against that day.*
> 2 Timothy 1:12

> *Thou therefore endure hardness, as a good soldier of Jesus Christ.*   2 Timothy 2:3

> *I endure all things for the elect's sakes, that they may also obtain the salvation which is in Christ Jesus with eternal glory.*
> 2 Timothy 2:10

> *If we suffer, we shall also reign with him.*
>
> 2 Timothy 2:12

> *Yea, and all that will live godly in Christ Jesus shall suffer persecution.* 2 Timothy 3:12

If we can only learn the lessons of Paul's life, we will find it easy to lay aside our feeble excuses, say "Yes, Lord," and begin to pay the price to see something happen in the twenty-first century. Excellence in ministry cost Paul long, lonely years of service. It cost him stripes, shipwreck, stoning, cold, nakedness, hunger and imprisonment. In the end, it cost him his life, but he gladly paid any price and thanked God that he was counted worthy to do so.

Paul was not some daredevil thrill-seeker going about asking for trouble. If he had been killed or imprisoned before his time, his ministry would never have reached out as it did. He was quite content to slip out of Damascus in a basket (see Acts 9:25) and out of Caesarea by ship (see Acts 9:30). After all, even Jesus slipped through crowds and escaped their wrath because His *"time"* was *"not yet come"* (John 7:6).

When Paul knew that both Jews and Gentiles of Iconium were preparing an assault to stone him, he fled to Lystra and Derbe (see Acts 14:5-6). When the

A Total Commitment

angry Jews at Thessalonica took Jason and another disciple as prisoners, Paul went away by night to Berea (see Acts 17:6-10). When these men followed him to Berea, he went away again — this time by sea (see Verses 13-14). When he learned that Jews were lying in wait for him in Syria, he changed his plans and went through Macedonia instead (see Acts 20:3). When he learned that forty Jews had conspired to kill him in Jerusalem, he sent his sister's son to tell the chief captain of the Roman army about it and to get him to intervene (Acts 23:12-22). When he was in danger of being returned to Jerusalem for trial, he appealed to Caesar (see Acts 25:9-12). Just as he never ran away from trouble in fear, Paul also never failed to recognize God's deliverance from trouble and His way of escape.

Persecution, in all its many forms, is one of the most extensive themes of the book of Acts. From the teaching on this subject, we learn many things. The most important of these things is that persecution always has a divine purpose and can always be turned to our own advantage and that of the Gospel.

God honored Paul for his willingness to face whatever life dealt him, and He still honors those who are willing to pay any price to do His will. He is still looking for men and women of total commitment. Halfhearted efforts have always produced halfhearted results, and they always will. Make that total commitment to God's will today, and begin to expect His excellence in your life.

Chapter 6

A Stubborn Determination

For Paul had determined to sail by Ephesus, because he would not spend the time in Asia: for he hasted, if it were possible for him, to be at Jerusalem the day of Pentecost.

Acts 20:16

And finding disciples, we tarried there seven days: who said to Paul through the Spirit, that he should not go up to Jerusalem. Acts 21:4

And as we tarried there many days, there came down from Judaea a certain prophet, named Agabus. And when he was come unto us, he took Paul's girdle, and bound his own hands and feet, and said, Thus saith the Holy Ghost, So shall the Jews at Jerusalem bind the man that owneth this girdle, and shall deliver him into the hands of the Gentiles. And when we heard these things, both we, and they of that place, besought him not to go up to Jerusalem. Acts 21:10-12

And when he would not be persuaded, we ceased, saying, The will of the Lord be done.
Acts 21:14

For some reason Paul felt that he should return to Jerusalem. He felt so strongly about it that he bypassed Ephesus and neglected Asia altogether, trying to complete his trip in time for the Feast of Pentecost. A mysterious chain of events unfolded, however, that caused many of his friends and, indeed, men of all succeeding generations, to wonder if Paul had not made a tragic mistake in insisting upon obedience to his inner urgings.

After bypassing Ephesus, Paul's company proceeded by ship to Miletus, Coos, Rhodes, Patara, past Cyprus and finally into Syria and the city of Tyre. It seems that Paul had no special reason for stopping in Tyre. Luke, Paul's companion and the

A Stubborn Determination

writer of the Acts of the Apostles, stated that the ship on which they sailed was to unload its cargo there. Perhaps Paul and his companions would not have even gone to Tyre if they had taken another ship. But they didn't take another ship. The Lord had His hand on Paul's life. He was guiding his every move. He brought him to Tyre so that He might speak to him there.

Whether or not any of the company had previous knowledge of a church in Tyre is not clear. Luke wrote:

> *And finding disciples, we tarried there seven days.* Acts 21:4

God used these Spirit-filled disciples of Tyre to speak to His servant Paul.

As Paul's company and the members of the church at Tyre had fellowship together in the Spirit, the Tyre disciples began to have some very strong feelings about Paul's trip, and they didn't hesitate to relay what they were feeling to Paul.

How this message was conveyed we cannot be sure. It may have come to these saints as a word of knowledge. It may have been in the form of a prophecy or an interpretation of a message in tongues. Other possibilities are unlimited, including dreams and visions.

The method is relatively unimportant. It was the message that was the important thing. These brethren perceived that Paul would face grave dangers if he persisted in going to Jerusalem, and this is what they told him.

Nothing more is said of the ten-day visit except that on the departure date the local disciples, with their wives and children, accompanied the party to the ship. There they all kneeled down together on the shore and prayed a final prayer — probably for Paul. He seemed undaunted in his purpose.

From Tyre, the ship sailed to Ptolemais, where Paul spent a day with the brethren to be found there, and then they proceeded to Caesarea the following day.

In Caesarea, Paul and his company were housed in the home of Philip the evangelist (familiar to all Bible lovers as the man responsible for the great Samaritan revival of Acts 8). Philip was now older, was widely recognized as an evangelist, and he had four unmarried daughters who all had exceptional gifts of prophecy. It was there in Philip's house that the Lord spoke to Paul again.

It was not by coincidence that at that very time, Agabus, a prophet of Judaea, decided to pay a visit to Caesarea. He was a true prophet of the Lord. The only other biblical reference to him is found in Acts 11. There it is recorded that he traveled with other

A Stubborn Determination

prophets from Jerusalem to Antioch. In Antioch, Agabus prophesied that there would be a great drought throughout the whole world. His words were inspired and true. The prophecy came to pass during the reign of the great Roman emperor, Claudius Caesar. Luke respected Agabus enough to relate every detail of his daring prophecies.

On this particular occasion, the prophecy was enacted in dramatic form, making its message clear and unmistakable. Agabus took Paul's girdle, the sash or belt tied around the waist of his robe, and with it, he bound Paul's hands and feet. As he did this, he declared:

> *Thus saith the Holy Ghost, So shall the Jews at Jerusalem bind the man that owneth this girdle, and shall deliver him into the hands of the Gentiles.* Acts 21:11

If these warnings were not enough to convince Paul, they were enough to convince his companions. Luke wrote:

> *And when we heard these things, both we, and they of that place, besought him not to go up to Jerusalem.* Acts 21:12

The *"we"* of this passage refers not only to Luke

but to the other members of the missionary party. *"They of that place"* refers to Philip, his four prophetess daughters, and other saints of Caesarea.

The tenseness of the situation was mounting. First, the disciples of Tyre gave their warning; then Agabus the prophet gave his warning. With this, Luke joined, Philip joined, the four daughters joined. And they all tried to persuade Paul not to go to Jerusalem.

These were not the only warnings that Paul received. While in Miletus, Paul spoke to the elders of Ephesus, whom he had called to that place. He said:

> *And now, behold, I go bound in the spirit unto Jerusalem, not knowing the things that shall befall me there: save that the Holy Ghost witnesseth in every city, saying that bonds and afflictions abide [await] me.*
> Acts 20:22-23

Not only did the disciples of Tyre warn him, not only did Agabus warn him, not only did Luke warn him, not only did Philip warn him, not only did four prophetesses warn him — he was warned by someone in every single city he entered. And still he would not pay heed to the multitude of these words:

A Stubborn Determination   111

He would not be persuaded.   Acts 21:14

When I was still a very young minister, I was reading a popular commentary on the book of Acts, and the author was saying that all the "trouble" that came to Paul in Jerusalem and the events that followed were a result of his disobedience to these warnings of prophecy. The author went so far as to suggest that Paul was probably backslidden at the time.

Did the Lord want Paul to go to Jerusalem or not? Was he right in insisting on going? Or was he wrong? Did he disobey the Holy Ghost? Did he bring unnecessary trouble upon himself?

Why should Paul even want to go to Jerusalem? He knew that the Jerusalem Jews hated him. Jews everywhere hated him. Had they not been plotting his death since the first day he began to name the name of Jesus? He knew that Jerusalem would be overrun with Jews during the Feast of Pentecost. What could have been his motive for going, a motive so strong that it caused him to decline the advice of even his Spirit-filled friends and colaborers? Just what was God's plan for Paul?

Immediately after Paul's conversion and during his three days of fasting, God spoke to Ananias:

But the Lord said unto him [Ananias], Go thy way: for he [Paul] is a chosen vessel unto

> *me, to bear my name before the Gentiles, and kings, and the children of Israel.* Acts 9:15

This word represented a thumbprint of God's plan for Paul's life: ministry to the Gentiles, to kings and to the Jewish people. Had Paul totally fulfilled that plan? Not yet! His first attempts to win fellow Jews failed, so Paul then turned to the Gentiles (Acts 22:18 and 21). Since that time he had remained a faithful witness to the Gentile nations, having become the recognized *"minister to the Gentiles,"* and having established many Gentile churches. This was a noble work. His success in this field, no doubt, influenced his friends to discourage a move in any other direction. Paul was needed.

But God had something else for Paul to do. He wanted Paul to carry the name of Jesus before kings and before the children of Israel in a greater way, and now some inner urging moved him toward Jerusalem. He knew it wasn't his own desire, that it was the urging of the Holy Spirit. He must get to Jerusalem. He must pass Ephesus and neglect Asia and rush to Jerusalem. The children of Israel from every nation would gather there, and God had chosen him to bear the name of the Lord Jesus Christ before them. He must not fail. He must hurry. He must not let anyone or anything stand in his way. He must be there during the Feast when all nations were represented.

A Stubborn Determination

Yes, he knew that he would be bound. That was part of God's plan. He would be delivered to the Gentiles. That was okay. He had been chosen to take them the message of Jesus too. Yes, he would be tried and imprisoned, but he had been chosen to go before kings and to tell them of Jesus. He was ready to be bound — and even to die if necessary — and no one could be allowed to stand in his way. He must get back to Jerusalem. The urgency in his spirit made him a very stubborn man.

The prophecy of Agabus to Paul was completely in agreement with what the Holy Spirit had been speaking in other cities. His method was moving, colorful and convincing, but what did he say? He said that the Jews would bind Paul and deliver him to the Gentiles. Those words were true, and they did come to pass. Agabus, however, did not tell Paul *not* to go to Jerusalem. He simply warned him of the things that would take place if he did go.

Jesus knew what would happen on the cross, but He went anyway, and Paul did the same. Agabus did not tell him anything that he didn't already know. He only confirmed the other messages he had been receiving all along the way.

The wording of Acts 21:4 has led many to believe that Paul was actually forbidden to go to Jerusalem. In a more literal sense it might read, *"We went and found the disciples [of Tyre] and stayed there a week, and they, warned by the Spirit, urged Paul to abandon his visit to Jerusalem."*

The Holy Ghost did not forbid Paul to go to Jerusalem. These good brethren of Tyre, knowing what was going to happen to Paul (because the Holy Spirit had shown them), urged him to change his mind. Men urged him to change his mind. Agabus, the disciples of Tyre, Luke, the rest of Paul's company, Philip and his daughters and the disciples of Caesarea all urged Paul to change his mind. But he refused. He couldn't listen to even his closest and most faithful companions. God was urging him on. He must get to Jerusalem. There was work to do there. He could not afford to let anyone stop him or hold him back.

Therefore, Paul's reply to all these urgings was:

> *None of these things move me, neither count I my life dear unto myself, so that I might finish my course with joy, and the ministry, which I have received of the Lord Jesus, to testify the gospel of the grace of God.* Acts 20:24

> *Why mean ye to weep and to break mine heart? for I am ready not to be bound only, but also to die at Jerusalem for the name of the Lord Jesus.* Acts 21:13

A Stubborn Determination

Paul knew what was coming, and he was ready for it, so no one could change his mind. He had one thought — *"the ministry"* — and with that, he walked into Jerusalem and into lion's lair. He was apprehended, mistreated and imprisoned. That day marked the end of his physical liberty and the beginning of a long chain of abuses that was to culminate in his losing his head in Rome.

Did he bring all this suffering upon himself needlessly? Was it the result of disobedience or backsliding? The proof to me that this is not the case and that he was obeying God is that the Lord Himself appeared to Paul in the prison in Jerusalem:

> *And the night following [trial before the council] the Lord stood by him, and said, Be of good cheer, Paul: for as thou hast testified of me in Jerusalem, so must thou bear witness also at Rome.* Acts 23:11

God doesn't talk like that to backsliders.

Less than one week after Paul entered the city of Jerusalem, he was captured by angry Jews. They were beating him and would have killed him on the spot, but Roman soldiers discovered it — because the entire city was in an uproar. They rescued him from the mob, bound him with two chains and were forced to carry him overhead into their palace headquarters to keep him alive.

As Paul was entering the Roman headquarters, he spoke to the chief captain of the band and asked permission to defend himself before the people. When the captain learned that Paul was not a criminal, he consented. Paul stood high on the palace steps, while the angry mob below shouted, *"Away with him"* (Acts 21:36). Paul then did something absolutely amazing:

> *Paul ... beckoned with the hand unto the people. And when there was made a great silence, he spake unto them in the Hebrew tongue.* Acts 21:40

There is something strange about this scene. Just a few minutes after this crowd had beaten Paul and even sought his death, they suddenly *"made a great silence"* and listened to him bring a message that took twenty-one verses to record (see Acts 22:1-21).

In his message, Paul recounted in detail his conversion experience on the Damascus road, the subsequent happenings in Damascus and his first visit to Jerusalem afterward. He reminded the crowd that he had once persecuted the Christians, beginning with his consent to Stephen's martyrdom. All the while, the people listened attentively.

A Stubborn Determination

Then, just as suddenly as it had begun, the silence ended. The Spirit of God had hovered over the crowd and quieted them to hear the message. Now that spell was broken:

> *They ... lifted up their voices, and said, Away with such a fellow from the earth: for it is not fit that he should live. And as they cried out, and cast off their clothes, and threw dust into the air, the chief captain commanded him to be brought into the castle, and bade that he should be examined by scourging; that he might know wherefore they cried so against him.* Acts 22:22-24

The next morning Paul was brought before the Jewish council. When he tried to defend himself, someone slapped him. The council meeting ended in such confusion that the chief captain, fearing that the Jewish leaders would pull Paul into pieces, again rescued him by force, taking him back to the castle. That night the Lord stood by him and spoke those comforting words: *"Be of good cheer, Paul: for as thou hast testified of me in Jerusalem, so must thou bear witness also at Rome."*

Paul had fulfilled his calling to the Jews. He was able to glorify Christ to representatives of all Judaism at one time. He should therefore *"be of good* *cheer," t*he Lord directed. It didn't matter that his friends had failed to understand his motivation. They meant well, but their understanding of God's purpose had been limited. They knew only in part. They had tried to discourage what would prove to be a blessing to all generations to come. For it was during periods of imprisonment that Paul found time to write his letters to the churches.

Paul knew the value of obedience to God. When his friends could not convince him to change his mind, they accepted his decision:

> *[They] ceased, saying, The will of the Lord be done.* Acts 21:14

And the will of the Lord was done, but only because Paul closed his ears to everything but the voice of God. Thank God for a man of stubborn determination who was not easily swayed by popular opinion. We need more such men and women today. You can be one of them.

Chapter 7

A Realistic Approach

Him [Timothy] would Paul have to go forth with him; and took and circumcised him because of the Jews which were in those quarters: for they knew all that his father was a Greek. Acts 16:3

Then Paul took the men, and the next day purifying himself with them entered into the temple, to signify the accomplishment of the days of purification, until that an offering should be offered for every one of them.
Acts 21:26

Paul seems to have mellowed through the years.

Don't we all! The idealism of youth is wonderful, but it must be tempered by realism, or we go through life butting heads with everyone around us. We are still living in an imperfect world, with imperfect people. The Church is still an imperfect Church, and the Lord loves it no less for that. Each one of us is lacking in perfection (a painful revelation for some). Therefore, we must not lose our idealism, but we must temper that idealism with reality.

Paul developed a very practical approach to life. He would, in all good conscience, serve the Lord personally as the Spirit guided him. But he would not expect that everyone live up to the same standard by which he personally lived. He would set the example, and it would be up to others to follow or not to follow.

Paul felt that he could take certain liberties in life, but if he thought for a moment that those liberties would in any way offend a brother or cause confusion, he would not insist on them. He would become *"all things to all people."* And if, by taking certain action that he found personally offensive, he could bring unity to the Body, he was willing to do that too.

I hesitate to use the word "compromise" in this discussion, for it has been a very dirty word for those of us who have wanted to please God and

A Realistic Approach

do His will. "Never compromise!" we were taught. Therefore, compromise, in our thinking, has always been linked to backsliding and to disobedience.

That is often true, but not always so. There are many compromises in the Christian life. The person who has never learned to compromise cannot have a successful marriage, for instance. The fathers and mothers who have never learned to compromise will alienate their children. The believer who cannot compromise with co-workers will lose many or most of them.

Paul learned to compromise when his personal sacrifice was for the greater good. There are several examples in Scripture. One of them concerned the circumcision of Timothy:

> *Him [Timothy] would Paul have to go forth with him; and took and circumcised him because of the Jews which were in those quarters: for they knew all that his father was a Greek.* Acts 16:3

That commentary I read as a young minister listed the circumcision of Timothy as "the first step in Paul's compromising backsliding." I can understand that such an act might appear on the surface to be a compromise. Paul had just won a great battle at the council of Jerusalem, and Acts 15 declared his victory over the legalizers. They had come saying:

> *Except ye be circumcised after the manner of Moses, ye cannot be saved.* Acts 15:1

Paul, Barnabas and James refuted this argument, holding that there was no need for Gentile converts to keep the Law. And they won their case. When Paul later wrote to the Gentile converts of Galatia, he stated:

> *Behold, I Paul say unto you, that if ye be circumcised, Christ shall profit you nothing.* Galatians 5:2

In Galatians 2, Paul openly condemned other leaders of the church because they wanted to circumcise Titus, a Greek. Then he turned around and circumcised Timothy! Why? Did he compromise? Did he backslide?

The difference, I believe, is that Timothy was not a Gentile convert. He was the son of a Jewess. Although she was married to a Greek, her son was still a legal Jew. Although Paul was against the circumcising of Gentile converts, he was never against the circumcising of his fellow Jews (see Romans 3:1).

Did Timothy have to be circumcised? Of course

A Realistic Approach

not. In Christ Jesus, *"neither circumcision availeth anything, nor uncircumcision."* Why then was Timothy circumcised? Paul explained his decision this way:

> *And unto the Jews I became as a Jew, that I might gain the Jews; to them that are under the law, as under the law, that I might gain them that are under the law; to them that are without law, as without law, (being not without law to God, but under the law to Christ,) that I might gain them that are without law. To the weak became I as weak, that I might gain the weak: I am made all things to all men, that I might by all means save some. And this I do for the gospel's sake, that I might be partaker thereof with you.*
>
> 1 Corinthians 9:20-23

Timothy had a good background for work among the Jewish people. He had been reared by a faithful Jewish mother and grandmother (see 2 Timothy 1:5). Lois and Eunice taught Timothy from a child the Holy Scriptures (see 2 Timothy 3:15). And he *"was well reported of by the brethren that were at Lystra and Iconium"* (Acts 16:2). Timothy had only one problem: he was from Asia Minor, and the Jews in

Asia Minor had a reputation for laziness and half-heartedness.

Timothy would never be well accepted among the orthodox Jews unless he was circumcised. The decision made in Jerusalem did not apply to him. He was a Jew, so Paul circumcised him and took him along. It is evident from the passage that the act was done for the sake of the Jews, not in fear of the Jews. These sacrificial efforts of Paul and Timothy were well rewarded. We read, *"and so were the churches established in the faith, and increased in number daily"* (Acts 16:5).

Another example of Paul's realistic approach to life with other brothers came much later in his life, at the end of that tumultuous journey back to Jerusalem:

> *Do therefore this that we say to thee: We have four men which have a vow on them; them take, and purify thyself with them, and be at charges with them, that they may shave their heads: and all may know that those things, whereof they were informed concerning thee, are nothing; but that thou thyself also walkest orderly, and keepest the law.*
>
> *Then Paul took the men, and the next day purifying himself with them entered into the temple, to signify the accomplishment of the*

A Realistic Approach

days of purification, until that an offering should be offered for every one of them.
Acts 21:23-24 and 26

The church leaders at Jerusalem asked Paul to go into the Temple, submit to a Jewish ceremony of purification and pay for four other men to complete their ceremonies. And he chose to do that.

Going into the Temple was no big deal. Early in the Acts of the Apostles we read of the disciples going frequently into the synagogues. It was there, in the place of worship and learning, that they found those who were hungry for truth. Jesus entered the synagogues and the Temple often.

The question is not, then, Why did Paul enter the Temple? The question is, Why did Paul submit himself to the purification ceremony? And why did he pay so that four Jewish-Christian men could have their heads shaved and have offerings given in their behalf? These acts seem contradictory to the balance of his teachings (see Acts 13:39, Romans 3:20, 7:4, 7:6, Galatians 2:16, 3:11, 5:18, Ephesians 2:15 and Colossians 2:14). What good purpose was served by this?

From the very beginning of his ministry, Paul had lacked the cooperation of the Jerusalem Church. The leadership distrusted him and did not cooperate with him. Because of their Jewish background, these men were prejudiced against his Gentile ministry. At times this attitude of the mother church hindered Paul's progress. Of a certainty, it never did his work any good.

Paul traced this attempted perversion of the Galatian converts to a Jerusalem source. He blamed Palestinian emissaries for introducing confusion and strife among the people of Corinth. In short, well-meaning church leaders from Jerusalem were not only hindering the spread of the Gospel, but were attempting to tear down what had already been done by introducing the Law as a must for salvation.

Not all Christians of Jerusalem were at fault. Peter, James and John, after differing with Paul on some issues of law, finally gave him their right hand of fellowship and agreed that he should go to the Gentiles (see Galatians 2:9). The trouble came from a certain, small, but powerful faction in the church which stirred up elements of discord. It was made up mainly of Pharisees striving to turn Christianity into a sect of Judaism. It was no secret that some of these factions had sent emissaries to Paul's Gentile groups, attempting to turn them away from him (see Galatians 2:4-5).

Although thousands had been converted in Jerusalem, many of them had been scattered due to persecution, and those who remained were, as a

A Realistic Approach

whole, traditional Jewish believers. They were *"all zealous of the law"* (Acts 21:20). The transition from Law to grace was a struggle for them, a struggle in which they had apparently made very little progress. All indications are that they had never matured beyond the point of looking upon Jesus only as the Jewish Messiah. They were yet babes, drinking the milk of Christianity, while still remaining burdened with the yoke of the Law.

James seems to have been divinely ordained as the apostle to this transitional church. He had a God-given ability to nurse these followers along. He was lenient with them, giving them the Gospel liberty of which Paul spoke (see 1 Corinthians 8:9), while seeking to prevent them from stumbling by trying to keep the Law.

Paul was likewise cautious in his dealings with them. He feared that if he fought their prejudices openly, they might perhaps renounce Christianity entirely and make shipwreck of their faith. He was afraid that if such young babies were disciplined, they would not understand why they were being corrected.

Due to this immaturity, the Jerusalem Church, as a whole, considered Paul to be a despiser of the Law, a reviler of traditions and a Hellenist — not a true Hebrew (see Acts 21:21). Paul no doubt hoped that his visit to Jerusalem would set things right with the church there. Once there, he endeavored, by the force of Christian love and forbearance, to win the hearts of those whom he regarded, despite their weaknesses and errors, as brethren in Christ and thus overcome the prejudices that had impeded his progress.

If he could win over that church to the truth of the New Testament liberty or avert its open hostilities to himself and his ministry, that would do more toward the spread of Christianity than the conversion of Ephesus. Indeed, if he failed in his mission, it would mean a permanent schism in the Body of Christ. He was ready gladly to adopt any lawful means to prevent that end.

During this particular Jerusalem visit Paul did several things to achieve these goals:

1. Paul brought an offering from the Gentile churches to the church at Jerusalem.

Why should the newly converted Gentile nations send an offering to the long-standing Jerusalem Church? This was nothing more than an act of Christian love and appreciation, and Paul encouraged the Gentiles to send the offering as their token of love to the mother church, in return for spiritual blessings received. Such a gift would surely reveal to the Jews that the love of God had been shed

A Realistic Approach

abroad in the hearts of heathen men (see Acts 24:17, Romans 15:25-26, 1 Corinthians 16:1-3 and 2 Corinthians 9:1-15).

2. Paul gave the Jerusalem Church a detailed account of his work among the Gentiles for the preceding four years.

When Peter reported his Gentile mission in Caesarea to this same skeptical church, they *"held their peace, and glorified God, saying, Then hath God also to the Gentiles granted repentance unto life"* (Acts 11:18). Paul's report gained the same enthusiastic response: *"And when they heard it, they glorified the Lord"* (Acts 21:20). This is exactly what Paul had been believing for. His prayers had been answered.

3. Paul willingly complied with the advice of the assembly that he enter the Temple, submit to Jewish purification and aid four other men in their vows. These acts removed all prejudices, disappointing the troublesome factions who had, no doubt, hoped Paul would refuse to do it.

The requirements were simple. His sojourn among Gentiles had rendered him unclean according to Jewish Law. He was thought to be as contaminated as if he had touched a dead body. To again be acceptable to the Jewish world, he must submit to purification ceremonies.

The Old Testament book of Numbers gives us a picture similar to Paul's case. Such simple cases required no more than the sprinkling of the water of separation before entering the Temple and washing the body and changing the clothes at the end of seven days (see Numbers 19:16 and 19 and Acts 21:26-27).

The case with the four men was different. They had taken upon themselves the Nazarite vow (see Numbers 6). It was customary for those who had received deliverance from any great peril or who desired to testify publicly to their dedication to God to take upon themselves this vow. This was one of the Jewish customs that was carried over by the early Jerusalem converts.

There was no set time limit for the vow. In the cases of Samuel, Samson and John the Baptist, it was observed for a lifetime. They drank no strong drink, kept their distance from dead bodies and let their hair grow long. Because they never ended the vow, they escaped many of the other observances that accompanied its consummation.

Others took the vow for a shorter period. A common period of thirty days is suggested by both the Talmud and the writings of the historian Josephus.

A Realistic Approach

At the end of thirty days, the man involved had to appear in the Temple and give sacrifices. His hair was cut and burned on the altar.

Several sacrifices were involved: a one-year-old male lamb (without blemish) for a burnt offering, a one-year-old ewe lamb (without blemish) for a sin offering, one ram (without blemish) for peace offerings, a basket of unleavened bread, cakes of fine flour mingled with oil, wafers of unleavened bread anointed with oil, a meat offering and various drink offerings (see Numbers 6).

Offerings such as these were obviously beyond the means of the poor. It was customary, therefore, for the rich, as an act of piety, to pay the necessary expenses for the poorer to complete their vows. There is nothing in the Scriptures to indicate that Paul was independently rich, and where he got the funds to sponsor these men can only be imagined. But he believed this to be a cause meriting the use of God's money.

The Roman ruler, Agrippa the First, had done this same thing with the Nazarites — just for popularity. Paul did it for peace. In all of this, Paul was not upholding the Judaizers who were attempting to place the Gentiles under the Law. He never gave them opportunity (see Galatians 2:5).

James did not approve of the Judaizers either. He

gave Paul the hand of fellowship. Still, both men used wisdom in their dealings. They were truly *"wise as serpents, and harmless as doves"* (Matthew 10:16), truly willing to be *"made all things to all men that [they] might by all means save some"* (1 Corinthians 9:22). To the Jews, they became as Jews (see 1 Corinthians 9:20).

When confronted with the division among the Roman believers over the issue of eating certain meats, Paul summarized his revelation in these words:

> *Let us not therefore judge one another any more: but judge this rather, that no man put a stumblingblock or an occasion to fall in his brother's way.* Romans 14:13

Paul knew better than anyone the probable consequences of his decisive actions in Jerusalem, but his great love made him willing to adopt even the most burdensome ceremonies if, by doing so, he could save a brother from falling. Although we have all been delivered from the bondage of the Law, we may sometimes be called upon to submit to its requirements in order to win someone to the Gospel.

Be careful! Some would have us believe that Paul's willingness to become all things to all people was a license to sin, and that is not the case. This truth

A Realistic Approach

also does not give us the right to disobey God. We are only talking about going the extra mile and carrying an additional burden to aid a brother in need or to save a lost soul.

Ask God to give you a realistic approach to life's problems and the complex issues of interpersonal relationships we face now in the twenty-first century. He has promised to hear and answer your prayer.

Chapter 8

A Secret Weapon

I will pray with the spirit, and I will pray with the understanding also: I will sing with the spirit, and I will sing with the understanding also.   1 Corinthians 14:15

I thank my God, I speak with tongues more than ye all.   1 Corinthians 14:18

Paul possessed a secret weapon. He called it praying *"with the spirit."* We know it simply as speaking in tongues.

When I first heard of speaking in tongues from some of the members of my high school Bible club, I was convinced that they were involved in something very dangerous and possibly satanic. Since I was the founder and president of the club, I felt it was my duty to study the matter and help to correct their thinking.

I found a book that agreed with my assessment and began learning its arguments so that I could help my "erring" classmates. When I felt that I was ready to "straighten them out" and approached them with the arguments I had memorized, I was surprised to notice that what I was telling them contained inconsistencies. So I decided to go back and study the matter more thoroughly.

This time, instead of using the book and the references it suggested, I read directly from the Bible. I was amazed to find that speaking in tongues was a very biblical experience which the early believers practiced and taught.

Isaiah had prophesied about the coming manifestation of speaking in tongues (see Isaiah 28:11). Just before He went back to Heaven, Jesus included speaking in tongues in His list of signs that He said would *"follow them that believe"* (Mark 16:17). The Acts of the Apostles records the fact that tongues were received every time the believers experienced the baptism of the Holy Spirit (see Acts 2:4-11, 10:44-46, and 19:6). And Paul dedicated three entire chapters of his first letter to the Corinthians to the uses and abuses of speaking in tongues (see 1 Corinthians 12-14).

A Secret Weapon

Rather than turn me off to the manifestation of speaking in tongues, my research created a hunger within me to receive the power promised to the early believers by Jesus and that seemed to include this sign (see Acts 1:8). I went on to receive the baptism of the Holy Spirit with the accompanying evidence of speaking in tongues, and my life was transformed by the experience. The edification gained through prayer in the Spirit enabled me to become a missionary and to minister in more than sixty nations.

Since one title in this Master Keys Series is dedicated entirely to this phenomenon of speaking in tongues (*Speaking in Tongues*, McDougal Publishing [Hagerstown, MD: 1988, 1997, 2000, 2010]), I will not repeat that material here. I cannot, however, write about the secrets of effectiveness in the life of the apostle Paul and ignore this all-important subject.

Paul didn't ignore speaking in tongues. No other subject merited more space in his writings to the churches. He himself spoke in tongues as praise and as intercession (see 1 Corinthians 14:14-15). He believed that this practice was edifying, and he recommended it to everyone (see 1 Corinthians 14:4-5). He used his ability to speak in tongues more than the Corinthian Christians (who were known for their abuse of the gift) (see 1 Corinthians 14:18). And he commanded us in his writings not to quench this supernatural experience (see 1 Corinthians 14:39).

If something has come to us so highly recommended by a man of Paul's stature, we must not take it lightly. Each of us must learn more about this experience, be sure to make it our own and use it well.

The most recent survey I am aware of shows that there are now more than half a billion believers worldwide who have been baptized in the Holy Spirit and spoken with other tongues. This is a growing percentage of the world's population, and it is also the beginning of the fulfillment of Joel's prophecy that God would pour out His Spirit *"upon all flesh"* (Joel 2:28).

But many of those who have received this Holy Spirit outpouring (including speaking in tongues) have not made full use of their gift. There are several reasons. Many have simply not been instructed. Even though they spoke in tongues when they were filled with the Spirit, they are not aware of the further applications of this gift — intercessory prayer in the Spirit and praise. They leave their new weapon stored in a safe place, glad to have it, but ignorant of its power.

The enemy of our souls, knowing the power of intercessory prayer and spiritual praise, has made a major effort to muddy the waters, causing as much

A Secret Weapon

confusion as possible about speaking in tongues, and leaving many with the fear of falling into error or even being used of the devil if they use this gift. Their weapons thus remain hidden.

Many have experimented with prayer in the Spirit and spiritual praise in tongues, only to back off when the enemy tells them, "You are accomplishing absolutely nothing. This is ridiculous. You are wasting your time. This is childish gibberish." Nobody wants to be wasting his or her time. Nobody wants to be doing something ridiculous. Nobody wants to work at something that accomplishes nothing. So after a short trial period (in which they increasingly get the feeling that they are wasting their time), many people stop speaking in tongues. And this utterly delights the enemy.

The simple fact that Satan is a master liar and the father of lies (see John 8:44) is one of the most important truths of the Scriptures. In order to defend ourselves against these lies we must arm ourselves with the powerful Word of God. The writings of Paul (which include his teachings on speaking in tongues) have been recognized by Church fathers for centuries to be part of the Holy Bible that shows us God's viewpoint on things. Let us accept God's viewpoint. Take your secret weapon out of its hiding place and use it for the glory of God!

As for the enemy's lie that speaking in tongues

is childish gibberish: It has been such an education for me to travel to so many countries and hear the people speaking in many languages. If I hadn't known they were adults carrying on a legitimate conversation I might have thought they were imitating birds or playing children's games. Languages are so varied, and so strange-sounding to those who do not know them, that they seem absurd, childish.

I remember standing in a monorail station in Japan in 1964 thinking that the announcer was saying the same thing over and over. He wasn't. The endings placed on certain words made it sound like repetition to me. A minister who accompanied me told me what was being said and cleared up my confusion.

If you didn't know English and you heard someone saying a simple phrase like, "The children were running and skipping and jumping," you might think the person was speaking nonsense. Don't let Satan lie to you about this experience. Experiments have been done with linguists examining the phrases spoken in tongues by humble believers, and those linguists have testified that they distinguished definite language patterns in what was being said.

Speaking in tongues is not childish. It is not ridiculous. It is not a waste of time. It is a powerful weapon of warfare. Used consistently it will put the enemy to flight.

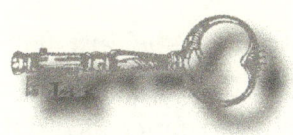

Chapter 9

A Life of Faith

And because he was of the same craft, he abode with them, and wrought: for by their occupation they were tentmakers. Acts 18:3

It is ironic that Paul and his tent making have been used by so many ministers as an excuse to divide themselves between secular work and Christian ministry. None of the Bible writers spoke more powerfully or convincingly of the life of faith than Paul, and none lived it more consistently and powerfully than he did.

Living by faith does not just mean living without a guaranteed income. It means depending on God as the Source of supply. In one sense, all believers live by faith, no matter how large their financial incomes. Many, who have good and stable incomes, take great leaps of faith when God speaks to them to do something special and beyond their means. Living by faith means that we are dependent on the Lord.

Ministers of the Gospel are called to live special lives of faith. In the Old Testament, the Levites did not receive an inheritance as did those of the other tribes. The inheritance of the Levites was spiritual. Physically, they lived from the tithes brought into the storehouse by the other Israelites. In a sense, we could say that they depended on the faithfulness of the other believers, but in a much greater sense (since they were serving God), He was responsible for them. They lived a life dependent on the Lord. If the other tribes did not obey God, He would supply the needs of the Levites in some other way.

Jesus taught His disciples a life of faith:

> *Then he called his twelve disciples together, and gave them power and authority over all devils, and to cure diseases. And he sent them to preach the kingdom of God, and to heal the sick. And he said unto them, Take nothing for your journey, neither staves, nor scrip, neither bread, neither money; neither have two coats apiece. And whatsoever house*

A Life of Faith

ye enter into, there abide, and thence depart. And whosoever will not receive you, when ye go out of that city, shake off the very dust from your feet for a testimony against them. And they departed, and went through the towns, preaching the gospel, and healing every where. Luke 9:1-6

Both Matthew and Mark give the same account (see Matthew 10:5-15 and Mark 6:7-11). When Jesus sent out the seventy, He gave them similar instructions:

After these things the Lord appointed other seventy also, and sent them two and two before his face into every city and place, whither he himself would come. Therefore said he unto them, The harvest truly is great, but the labourers are few: pray ye therefore the Lord of the harvest, that He would send forth labourers into his harvest. Go your ways: behold, I send you forth as lambs among wolves. Carry neither purse, nor scrip, nor shoes: and salute no man by the way.

And into whatsoever house ye enter, first say, Peace be to this house. And if the son of peace be there, your peace shall rest upon it: if not, it shall turn to you again. And in the same house remain, eating and drinking such things as they give: for the labourer is worthy of his hire. Go not from house to house.

And into whatsoever city ye enter, and they receive you, eat such things as are set before you: and heal the sick that are therein, and say unto them, The kingdom of God is come nigh unto you. But into whatsoever city ye enter, and they receive you not, go your ways out into the streets of the same, and say, Even the very dust of your city, which cleaveth on us, we do wipe off against you: notwithstanding be ye sure of this, that the kingdom of God is come nigh unto you. Luke 10:1-12

Paul taught the same thing:

Who goeth a warfare any time at his own charges? who planteth a vineyard, and eateth not of the fruit thereof? or who feedeth a flock, and eateth not of the milk of the flock? say I these things as a man? or saith not the Law the same also? For it is written in the law of Moses, thou shalt not muzzle the mouth of the ox that treadeth out the corn. Doth God take care for oxen? or saith he it altogether for our sakes? For our sakes, no doubt, this is written: that he that ploweth should plow in hope;

A Life of Faith

and that he that thresheth in hope should be partaker of his hope. If we have sown unto you spiritual things, is it a great thing if we shall reap your carnal things?

Do ye not know that they which minister about holy things live of the things of the temple? and they which wait at the altar are partakers with the altar? Even so hath the Lord ordained that they which preach the gospel should live of the gospel.

1 Corinthians 9:7-11 and 13-14

For the scripture saith, Thou shalt not muzzle the ox that treadeth out the corn. And, The labourer is worthy of his reward.

1 Timothy 5:18

God delights in supplying the needs of His servants through His people (see Luke 6:38). He uses this means as a double blessing. The needs of His servants are met, and in the process, His people are blessed for their faithfulness.

It is very likely that the prophet Elijah was criticized when he "imposed himself" upon the starving widow of Zarephath and demanded her last bit of meal for himself (see 1 Kings 17:8-16). I have no doubt, however, that this widow thanked God every day during the months that followed as she and her son were sustained by His miracles, while others around them perished from the famine.

The life of faith outlined in the Bible is clearly the will of God for His servants. Still, despite this knowledge, Paul sewed tents. Why? Did he intend to use the tents in his Asian evangelism? Apparently not.

In his first letter to the Corinthians, Paul spoke of his right not to work (in the secular sense):

> *Or I only and Barnabas, have not we power to forbear working?*   1 Corinthians 9:6

Paul did not use this right while in Corinth, however, thinking that it would be a hindrance to his ministry there:

> *If others be partakers of this power over you, are not we rather? Nevertheless we have not used this power; but suffer all things, lest we should hinder the gospel of Christ.*
> 1 Corinthians 9:12

Paul felt so strongly about this on that particular occasion that he said he would rather die than take money from the Corinthians:

> *But I have used none of these things: neither have I written these things, that it should be*

A Life of Faith

> *so done unto me: for it were better for me to die, than that any man should make my glorying void.*   1 Corinthians 9:15

He was determined to make the Gospel *"without charge"*:

> *What is my reward then? Verily that, when I preach the gospel, I may make the gospel of Christ without charge, that I abuse not my power in the gospel.*   1 Corinthians 9:18

At the same time Paul was refusing to take money from the Corinthians, he was accepting offerings from other churches, to the point of feeling that it was too much, that he had *"robbed"* them:

> *Have I committed an offence in abasing myself that ye might be exalted, because I have preached to you the gospel of God freely? I robbed other churches, taking wages of them, to do you service. And when I was present with you, and wanted, I was chargeable to no man: for that which was lacking to me the brethren which came from Macedonia supplied: and in all things I have kept myself from being burdensome unto you, and so will I keep myself. As the truth of Christ is in me,*

> *no man shall stop me of this boasting in the regions of Achaia.*   2 Corinthians 11:7-10

It wouldn't make sense to receive *"wages"* from one church to serve another and refuse to accept anything from the second, unless there was some other underlying problem. I am sure that was the case in Corinth.

The root of this matter seems to me to be the fact that insincere ministers had visited Corinth on occasion. They had tried to exalt themselves and to put Paul down. His love for the Corinthians made him bold to write a letter of clarification to them:

> *I think to be bold against some, which think of us as if we walked according to the flesh.*
>   2 Corinthians 10:2

In this second letter to the Corinthians (Chapters 10 through 12), Paul brought to light the foolish attitude of the false brethren of which he spoke. In doing so, he boasted of his own achievements. Part of what he said there was:

> *I am become a fool in glorying; ye have compelled me.*   2 Corinthians 12:11

One of Paul's boasts was that he, unlike others,

A Life of Faith

had not been chargeable to the Corinthians for his service to them in the Gospel. He had given them the Gospel without charge. But why did he make such a point of this?

It is evident to me that the *"false apostles"* of verse 13 of chapter 11 had done one of two things. Either they had abused the generosity of the Corinthians, or they had taken nothing and criticized those who did as having walked in the flesh. Either of these acts could have sparked Paul's response. He depended on God to supply his needs. If his needs could not be supplied in the normal way (through the people to whom he was ministering), God would make another way.

This principle had also been proven throughout the Scriptures. When there were no stores in the wilderness from which to buy, God sent manna down from Heaven (see Deuteronomy 2:7). When the people to whom Elijah ministered could no longer supply his needs because of a famine, God sent ravens to feed him (see 1 Kings 17:6). When the brook he was drinking from dried up, God multiplied the meal in a widow's barrel and the oil in her cruse to continue to meet the prophet's physical needs (see Verse 16). When it was too far and too late to send the multitudes that followed Him for food, Jesus multiplied loaves and fishes and fed them (see Matthew 14:15-21).

Paul's teaching to the Philippians on this subject has become the classic promise from God's Word on this subject for many of us:

> *But my God shall supply all your need according to his riches in glory by Christ Jesus.*
> Philippians 4:19

The life of faith is a wonderful one because depending on the Lord is wonderful. He never fails. His provision does not depend on the obedience of men. He is not affected by the weather, by the mail service or by any other outside circumstance. When we trust God, we no longer have to worry about being people pleasers. We can concentrate on doing the will of God. No man set a greater example than Paul did. Follow his example, and develop your own life of faith.

Chapter 10

A Man, But What A Man!

Serving the Lord with all humility of mind, and with many tears, and temptations, which befell me by the lying in wait of the Jews.

Acts 20:19

And I was with you in weakness, and in fear, and in much trembling. 1 Corinthians 2:3

For we would not, brethren, have you ignorant of our trouble which came to us in Asia, that we were pressed out of measure, above strength, insomuch that we despaired even of life. 2 Corinthians 1:8

> *For when we were come into Macedonia, our flesh had no rest, but we were troubled on every side; without were fightings, within were fears.* 2 Corinthians 7:5

Paul was not perfect or infallible. He was a great man, but he was a man. And no man (or woman) is infallible. Even if a person is a pope, president, prime minister, premier, prophet, priest, pastor or principal, he or she is still human. Men and women have passions, and men and women have limitations.

Despite his conversion, despite his calling, despite his revelation, despite his anointing, despite his labors, Paul remained a man until the day he died. He was flesh and was constantly struggling to keep that flesh in subjection to the Spirit of God. Beneath his outer skin lay the old nature of Saul of Tarsus, struggling to live again and be seen.

The overall life of Paul appears almost unrealistic in its mastery of the spiritual walk. Still, dispersed throughout the Scriptures are several short, but revealing glimpses of him as a man. Let us now take a look at some of them:

> *And Paul, earnestly beholding the council, said, Men and brethren, I have lived in all good conscience before God until this day.*

A Man, But What A Man!

> *And the high priest Ananias commanded them that stood by him to smite him on the mouth. Then said Paul unto him, God shall smite thee, thou whited wall: for sittest thou to judge me after the law, and commandest me to be smitten contrary to the law? And they that stood by said, revilest thou God's high priest? Then said Paul, I wist not, brethren, that he was the high priest: for it is written, Thou shalt not speak evil of the ruler of thy people.*   Acts 23:1-5

On a sudden impulse, Paul spoke out the powerful words of verse three. He spoke, not through hope of personal vengeance, but under inspiration of the Holy Spirit. The words that spouted from his lips were divinely ordained prophecy. God did smite Ananias. He was murdered by terrorists at the beginning of the Jewish War in AD 58. (This passage is similar to John 18:19-24, where Jesus received identical treatment for speaking boldly to the high priest.)

Paul's humanity does show through here. After speaking in this way by inspiration and anointing, he apologized, thinking that he had spoken out of his own spirit. He suddenly questioned his own prophetic revelation. His arrest and severe mistreatment could possibly have shaken his faith for a moment. This may be the very reason the Lord stood by him that same night in his cell and comforted him with the knowledge that he was in the will of God.

John the Baptist had a similar experience. After introducing Jesus to the people of Judaea as *"the Lamb of God who taketh away the sins of the world"* (1 John 1:29), he experienced periods of doubt during his imprisonment (see Matthew 11:2-3). When he sent emissaries to ask if Jesus was really the hoped-for Messiah or if they should look for another, Jesus did not answer with a rebuke. He said:

> *Go and shew John again those things which ye do hear and see: the blind receive their sight, and the lame walk, the lepers are cleansed, and the deaf hear, the dead are raised up, and the poor have the gospel preached to them. And blessed is he, whosoever shall not be offended in me.*
>
> Matthew 11:4-6

How comforting it is to know that God understands human frailties.

§

But I determined this with myself, that I

A Man, But What A Man!

> *would not come again to you in heaviness. For out of much affliction and anguish of heart I wrote unto you with many tears; not that ye should be grieved, but that ye might know the love which I have more abundantly unto you.*   2 Corinthians 2:1 and 4
>
> *For though I made you sorry with a letter, I do not repent, though I did repent: for I perceive that the same epistle hath made you sorry, though it were but for a season. Now I rejoice, not that ye were made sorry, but that ye sorrowed to repentance: for ye were made sorry after a godly manner, that ye might receive damage by us in nothing. For godly sorrow worketh repentance to salvation not to be repented of: but the sorrow of the world worketh death.*   2 Corinthians 7:8-10

Paul felt compelled to write a very grievous letter to his converts at Corinth. He condemned their disunity (1 Corinthians, chapter 1), their lack of spiritual growth (chapter 3), their loose moral standards (chapter 5), their habit of taking a brother to law (chapter 6), their lust and idolatry (chapter 6), their abuse of the Lord's Supper (chapter 11), their abuse of spiritual gifts (chapters 12 through 14) and their lack of faith in the resurrection (chapter 15).

Then, he felt condemned for being so harsh with the Corinthians and repented of the writings.

This should not surprise us, for discipline is difficult for any parent. The writings were, of course, justified. Paul was *"moved by the Spirit"* to write the words found in it. It was a word from God, His perfect mind for the Corinthians, and it has also become part of the Holy Bible, God's recognized Word to all generations. In the same letter Paul said:

> *But when we are judged, we are chastened of the Lord, that we should not be condemned with the world.*   1 Corinthians 11:32

Many of us believe that Paul also wrote the letter to the Hebrews. It declares:

> *For whom the Lord loveth He chasteneth, and scourgeth every son whom He receiveth.*   Hebrews 12:6

Paul knew well the admonition of the Law:

> *Thou shalt also consider in thine heart, that, as a man chasteneth his son, so the LORD thy God chasteneth thee.*   Deuteronomy 8:5

Paul also knew the wisdom of Solomon:

A Man, But What A Man!

> *My son, despise not the chastening of the* L<small>ORD</small>*; neither be weary of his correction. For whom the* L<small>ORD</small> *loveth he correcteth; even as a father the son in whom he delighteth.*
>
> Proverbs 3:11-12

How long it took Paul to realize his mistake regarding the letter to the Corinthians we cannot be sure. Why he ever doubted the inspiration of his words is also a mystery. We can only conclude that Paul was human and we humans make mistakes.

Paul did eventually hear from Heaven on this matter, and when he did, he repented because he had repented. He had been right in the first place. Knowing this, he went so far as to *"rejoice"* about the whole matter because the Corinthians *"sorrowed to repentance."*

§

> *Ye know how through infirmity of the flesh I preached the gospel unto you at the first. And my temptation which was in my flesh ye despised not, nor rejected; but received me as an angel of God, even as Christ Jesus.*
>
> Galatians 4:13-14

Paul had some temptation that was so grievous he called it an *"infirmity of the flesh."* It was no secret, and he seemed to be surprised that the Galatians had not despised or rejected him because of the severity of the temptation. Instead, they had received him in the gracious manner he describes.

Perhaps this grievous temptation was the result of the *"messenger of Satan"* or *"thorn in the flesh"* which buffeted Paul and about which he spoke on other occasions:

> *And lest I should be exalted above measure through the abundance of the revelations, there was given to me a thorn in the flesh, the messenger of Satan to buffet me, lest I should be exalted above measure. For this thing I besought the Lord thrice, that it might depart from me. And he said unto me, My grace is sufficient for thee: for my strength is made perfect in weakness. Most gladly therefore will I rather glory in my infirmities, that the power of Christ may rest upon me.*
>
> 2 Corinthians 12:7-9

A *"messenger of Satan"* was allowed to *"buffet"* Paul so that he would not become proud. Every man and woman alive has a tendency toward pride, and we often need God's help to overcome this tendency. Satan did not send this messenger to buffet Paul. Satan would have delighted in Paul being *"exalted

A Man, But What A Man!

above measure." God allowed this messenger of Satan to buffet Paul.

At first, Paul didn't like what was happening to him. That was a very human reaction. He saw this thing as a hindrance to progress, not as a check on his own ego. Three times he pleaded with the Lord to remove it, but the Lord knew that it was for Paul's good to let it remain. He supplied Paul grace to overcome it. Paul accepted the Lord's will, and decided to glory in his infirmities.

He should have been happy, for God mercifully spared him from the sin which marks the downfall of many great men and women of God. When pride creeps in, the power of God creeps out. When we cease to recognize that without Him we are nothing and without Him we can do nothing, God cannot continue to use us. Further use would only do us harm. He shows us His strength when we recognize our weakness.

§

> *And I baptized also the household of Stephanas: besides, I know not whether I baptized any other.*   1 Corinthians 1:16

It should be encouraging to all of us to note that Paul had a bad memory. His first statement was that he baptized none except Crispus and Gaius (see

Verse 14). After a moment's thought, he remembered baptizing also the family of Stephanas, but could not remember if he had baptized any others. There is hope for all of us.

§

> *And from thence, when the brethren heard of us, they came to meet us as far as Appii forum, and The three taverns: whom when Paul saw, he thanked God, and took courage.* Acts 28:15

If Paul *"took courage"* or "was encouraged," there must have been an element of discouragement there. The sight of brothers in a strange and menacing place encouraged him. We all need encouragement. We all need brothers and sisters to help us sometimes.

§

> *Now when they had gone throughout Phrygia and the region of Galatia, and were forbidden of the Holy Ghost to preach the word in Asia, after they were come to Mysia, they assayed to go into Bithynia: but the Spirit suffered them not.* Acts 16:6-7

Paul and his companions wanted to go to Asia.

A Man, But What A Man!   161

When the Holy Ghost forbade that, they tried to go to Bithynia. When *"the Spirit suffered them not,"* they went to Troas (see Verse 8). It was there that Paul had a vision in which God showed him where He did want him to go — Macedonia.

Paul's heart was honest. He didn't always know exactly what he should be doing, but he wanted to know. The Spirit mercifully closed certain doors and impeded other intended activities, and then the clear answer came for God's direction.

§

Things didn't always run smoothly for Paul. He was mistreated at every turn. He suffered inhuman consequences for the good he did in preaching the Gospel. Others tried to tear down the work he did. He suffered grievous temptations and a *"thorn in the flesh"* — a messenger of Satan sent to buffet him. His plans were often disrupted by mob violence, attempts on his life or lack of cooperation on the part of fellow Christians. When he desired to go to Thessalonica, *"Satan hindered"* him (1 Thessalonians 2:18). He suffered *"afflictions," "necessities, "distresses," "stipes," "imprisonments," "tumults" and "labours"* — to mention just a few of the difficulties he faced (2 Corinthians 6:4-5).

Paul was so opposed by a few men that he was forced to turn them over to Satan for the destruction of the flesh (see 1 Timothy 1:20). Although *"a great door"* was opened to him, there were *"many adversaries"* (1 Corinthians 16:9). He wasn't able to go everywhere that he *"purposed"* to go (see Acts 16:6-7, 19:21, 20:3 and Romans 1:13).

As we look back at the total picture, of which Paul saw only pieces here and there, and those not yet fit together, it now seems evident that many of the "hindrances" he experienced were actually blessings in disguise. They proved to be for his own good and for the good of the Gospel. His *"thorn in the flesh,"* for instance, was a master blessing. Constant persecution from unbelievers kept Paul reaching for more of God, and persecution from believers caused him to depend totally upon the Lord.

In the very same way, many of the things we consider to be hindrances in our lives are actually sent from Heaven for our good. Give thanks to God in everything.

Paul was not infallible, and no one knew that fact better than he did. In his latter years, he was still striving to know Christ fully. He said:

> *That I may know him, and the power of his resurrection, and the fellowship of his suffering, being made conformable unto His death … .*
> Philippians 3:10

A Man, But What A Man!

Paul was a man, but not just any man. He was a man transformed by the saving grace of Jesus Christ through a genuine conversion. He was a man who, from the first day of his new life in Christ, was motivated by a compelling zeal. He was a man who exhibited confidence and authority because of his recognized calling. He was a man with an eye single to the glory of God, who could stand alone, if necessary, because he had a divine revelation. He was a man who never looked back, because he had made a total commitment to God's ways. He was a man who was not moved by public opinion, because he had a stubborn determination to do the perfect will of God. He was a man who could get along with his fellow workers, because he had a realistic approach to life and ministry, even thought he never used his Christian liberty as a license to sin. He was a man possessed of a secret weapon, prayer in the Spirit. He was a man who was never moved by financial considerations, for he developed and taught a life of faith, dependence on the Lord as his Source.

Yes, Paul was a man. But, what a man!

Index

1 Corinthians 1 155
1 Corinthians 1:11 77
1 Corinthians 1:14 160
1 Corinthians 1:16 159
1 Corinthians 2:3 151
1 Corinthians 3 155
1 Corinthians 5 155
1 Corinthians 6 155
1 Corinthians 8:9 127
1 Corinthians 9:1 37
1 Corinthians 9:6 146
1 Corinthians 9:7-11 145
1 Corinthians 9:12 146
1 Corinthians 9:13-14 145
1 Corinthians 9:15 147
1 Corinthians 9:18 147
1 Corinthians 9:20 132
1 Corinthians 9:20-23 123
1 Corinthians 9:22 132
1 Corinthians 11 155
1 Corinthians 11:23 78
1 Corinthians 11:32 156
1 Corinthians 12-14 136, 155
1 Corinthians 14:4-5 137
1 Corinthians 14:14-15 137
1 Corinthians 14:15 135
1 Corinthians 14:18 135, 137
1 Corinthians 14:39 138
1 Corinthians 15 155
1 Corinthians 15:3-4 48
1 Corinthians 15:5 48, 56
1 Corinthians 15:6 49
1 Corinthians 15:7 49, 50
1 Corinthians 15:8 50
1 Corinthians 15:8-10 37
1 Corinthians 15:9 37
1 Corinthians 15:9-10 53
1 Corinthians 15:10 12, 171
1 Corinthians 15:51 11
1 Corinthians 16:1-3 129
1 Corinthians 16:9 162
1 John 1:29 154
1 Kings 17:6 149
1 Kings 17:8-16 145
1 Kings 17:16 149
1 Thessalonians 2:18 161
1 Thessalonians 5:18 100
1 Timothy 1:13 14, 15
1 Timothy 1:14 15
1 Timothy 1:15 15
1 Timothy 1:20 162
1 Timothy 2:7 38
1 Timothy 3:2-12 18
1 Timothy 5:18 145
2 Corinthians 1:8 151
2 Corinthians 2:1 155
2 Corinthians 2:4 155
2 Corinthians 5:17 13, 17
2 Corinthians 6:4-5 161
2 Corinthians 7:5 152
2 Corinthians 7:8-10 155
2 Corinthians 9:1-15 129
2 Corinthians 10:2 148
2 Corinthians 10-12 148
2 Corinthians 11:5 37
2 Corinthians 11:7-10 148
2 Corinthians 11:18 98
2 Corinthians 11:21 98

2 Corinthians 11:23   98
2 Corinthians 11:24-28   98
2 Corinthians 11:28   54
2 Corinthians 11:32   22
2 Corinthians 12:7-9   158
2 Corinthians 12:11   54, 148
2 Corinthians 13:2   78
2 Timothy 1:5   123
2 Timothy 1:7-8   101
2 Timothy 1:12   101
2 Timothy 2:3   101
2 Timothy 2:10   101
2 Timothy 2:12   102
2 Timothy 3:12   102
2 Timothy 3:15   123

A

Acts 1:3   46
Acts 1:8   76, 137
Acts 1:15   56
Acts 1:22   48
Acts 2:4-11   136
Acts 2:14   56
Acts 2:41   56
Acts 3:4-6   56
Acts 3:12   56
Acts 3:19   18
Acts 4:8   56
Acts 4:13   56
Acts 4:19   56
Acts 4:36   65, 76
Acts 4:37   65
Acts 5:3   56
Acts 5:9   56
Acts 5:15   56
Acts 5:36   39
Acts 5:37   39

Acts 6:9   27
Acts 6:10   27
Acts 6:11   27
Acts 7:54   28
Acts 7:57-58   28
Acts 7:58   29
Acts 8   38, 108
Acts 8:1   14, 29, 30
Acts 8:3   30
Acts 8:9   38
Acts 8:10   39
Acts 9:1-2   14, 30
Acts 9:3-7   82
Acts 9:6   83
Acts 9:8-9   82
Acts 9:10   83
Acts 9:11   83
Acts 9:12   83
Acts 9:13-14   83
Acts 9:15   112
Acts 9:15-16   83
Acts 9:16   81
Acts 9:19   24
Acts 9:20   21, 24
Acts 9:21   25
Acts 9:22   25
Acts 9:23   22, 25
Acts 9:25   102
Acts 9:27   65
Acts 9:28   31
Acts 9:29   27, 31, 32
Acts 9:29-31   21
Acts 9:30   102
Acts 9:31   34
Acts 9:32-35   57
Acts 9:40   57
Acts 10:5   57

Index of Scripture Portions Used

Acts 10:12   58
Acts 10:13   58
Acts 10:14   58
Acts 10:15   58
Acts 10:19-20   60
Acts 10:23   63
Acts 10:24   63
Acts 10:28   64
Acts 10:30-33   63
Acts 10:34   63, 64
Acts 10:35   64
Acts 10:36   64
Acts 10:44   63
Acts 10:44-46   136
Acts 10:45   63
Acts 11:12   63
Acts 11:18   129
Acts 11:24   70
Acts 11:25-26   22
Acts 11:26   35, 66
Acts 12:2   71
Acts 12:7-11   57
Acts 13:2   66
Acts 13:6-12   67
Acts 13:14-49   67
Acts 13:39   125
Acts 14:5-6   102
Acts 14:8-10   67
Acts 14:11   67
Acts 14:12   67
Acts 14:13   68
Acts 15   122
Acts 15:1   122
Acts 15:39   68
Acts 16:2   123
Acts 16:3   119, 121
Acts 16:5   124

Acts 16:6-7   160, 162
Acts 16:8   161
Acts 17:6-10   103
Acts 17:13-14   103
Acts 18:3   141
Acts 19:6   136
Acts 19:11-12   11
Acts 19:21   162
Acts 20:3   103, 162
Acts 20:16   105
Acts 20:19   151
Acts 20:22-23   95, 110
Acts 20:24   81, 96, 114
Acts 21:4   105, 107, 113
Acts 21:10-12   106
Acts 21:11   109
Acts 21:12   109
Acts 21:13   114
Acts 21:14   106, 111, 118
Acts 21:20   127, 129
Acts 21:21   127
Acts 21:23-24   125
Acts 21:26   119, 125
Acts 21:26-27   130
Acts 21:36   116
Acts 21:40   116
Acts 22:1-21   116
Acts 22:18   112
Acts 22:19   13
Acts 22:21   112
Acts 22:22-24   117
Acts 23:1-5   153
Acts 23:6   76
Acts 23:11   115
Acts 23:12-22   103
Acts 24:17   129
Acts 25:9-12   103

Acts 26:5   76
Acts 26:10-11   14
Acts 28:15   160

C

Colossians 1:24   100
Colossians 2:14   125

D

Daniel 7:14   75
Deuteronomy 2:7   149
Deuteronomy 8:5   156

E

Ephesians 2:15   125
Ephesians 5:20   100
Ephesians 6:18-19   11

G

Galatians 1:6   78
Galatians 1:12   26
Galatians 1:13   14
Galatians 1:14   77
Galatians 1:18-19   31
Galatians 1:22-24   34
Galatians 2:2   72, 78
Galatians 2:3   72
Galatians 2:4   71
Galatians 2:4-5   126
Galatians 2:5   72, 131
Galatians 2:6-7   73
Galatians 2:9   73, 126
Galatians 2:11   64
Galatians 2:12   64
Galatians 2:13   70
Galatians 2:14   74
Galatians 2:16   125
Galatians 3:11   125
Galatians 4:13-14   157
Galatians 5:1   72
Galatians 5:2   122
Galatians 5:18   125
Galatians 6:14   99
Genesis 22:18   75

H

Hebrews 12:6   156
Hosea 2:23   75

I

Isaiah 9:2   75
Isaiah 28:11   136
Isaiah 49:6   75
Isaiah 53:5   45
Isaiah 60:3   75

J

Joel 2:28   138
John 6:35   41
John 6:71   49
John 7:6   102
John 8:12   42
John 8:44   139
John 10:7   41
John 11:25   42
John 14:6   42
John 17:1   45
John 17:4   45
John 18:19-24   153
John 19:30   45
John 20:6   56
John 20:24   49

Index of Scripture Portions Used

John 20:24-29   71
John 20:28   47
John 20:30   47
John 21:2-3   62
John 21:3   62
John 21:4   62
John 21:6   62
John 21:7   62
John 21:15   56
John 21:16   56
John 21:20   70

L

Luke 4:15   75
Luke 4:22   40
Luke 4:36   40
Luke 4:39   55
Luke 4:44   75
Luke 5:1-3   61
Luke 5:3-6   55
Luke 5:4   61
Luke 5:5   61
Luke 5:6-7   62
Luke 5:7   70
Luke 5:10   70
Luke 5:26   41
Luke 6:38   145
Luke 7:49   41
Luke 8   71
Luke 8:25   41
Luke 8:51   55
Luke 9:1-6   143
Luke 9:28-29   55
Luke 10:1-12   144
Luke 22:14   49
Luke 22:30   38
Luke 22:31-32   55

Luke 22:47   49
Luke 24:12   56
Luke 24:34   48, 56

M

Mark 1:30-31   55
Mark 1:39   75
Mark 2:12   41
Mark 5:37   55, 71
Mark 6:2   41
Mark 6:7-11   143
Mark 7:27   75
Mark 7:37   41
Mark 9:2   55
Mark 14   71
Mark 14:10   49
Mark 14:17   49
Mark 14:33   55
Mark 16:10   46
Mark 16:11   46
Mark 16:15   76
Mark 16:17   136
Matthew 4:19   42
Matthew 4:23   75
Matthew 5-7   71
Matthew 8:7   75
Matthew 8:10   75
Matthew 8:14-15   55
Matthew 8:16   42
Matthew 8:22   42
Matthew 9:33   41
Matthew 9:35   75
Matthew 10:5   75
Matthew 10:5-15   143
Matthew 10:16   132
Matthew 11:2-3   154
Matthew 11:4-6   154

Matthew 13:54   40
Matthew 14:15-21   149
Matthew 14:29   55
Matthew 14:36   42
Matthew 15:21   75
Matthew 15:22-28   75
Matthew 15:26   75
Matthew 16:15   55
Matthew 16:16   55
Matthew 16:17   55
Matthew 16:19   55
Matthew 17:1   71
Matthew 17:1-2   55
Matthew 17:1-3   71
Matthew 17:27   55
Matthew 18:3   18
Matthew 19:21   43
Matthew 19:28   38
Matthew 26:8   5
Matthew 26:20   49
Matthew 26:37   55
Matthew 26:47   49
Matthew 28:2   44
Matthew 28:19   76

N

Numbers 6   130, 131
Numbers 19:16   130
Numbers 19:19   130

P

Philippians 3:5   76
Philippians 3:10   162
Philippians 4:13   100
Philippians 4:19   150
Proverbs 3:11-12   157
Psalm 22:27   75
Psalm 86:9   75

R

Romans 1:1   37
Romans 1:13   162
Romans 3:1   122
Romans 3:20   125
Romans 7:4   125
Romans 7:6   125
Romans 8:18   99
Romans 11:1   76
Romans 11:13   37
Romans 14:13   132
Romans 15:25-26   129
Romans 16:25-26   11

But by the grace of God I am what I am: and his grace which was bestowed upon me was not in vain; but I laboured more abundantly than they all: yet not I, but the grace of God which was with me.

1 Corinthians 15:10

www.ingramcontent.com/pod-product-compliance
Lightning Source LLC
Chambersburg PA
CBHW032120090426
42743CB00007B/407